PRAISE FOR FROM THE BADGE TO THE VINE

Not everyone will embrace ayahuasca as a legitimate healing tool—and that's okay. What this book does, through fearless and grounded storytelling, is move the conversation out of the shadows and into honest, meaningful territory. It did for me.

What makes this work especially valuable is its credibility with first responders—the most skeptical, battle-hardened among us. From the Badge to the Vine offers a clear, responsible lens on ayahuasca's potential role in healing. Well done.

-Dan Cronin, Deputy Assistant Director of High Threat Programs, U.S. Department of State, Diplomatic Security Service (DSS Ret.)

Kemmi Sadler spent twenty-six years carrying a badge and a gun. She enforced the very laws that kept her from the medicine that would eventually save her life. *From the Badge to the Vine* is an honest, raw testimony from a first responder who finally stopped pushing through and started healing.

-Matt Zemon, DMin, MSc, author of The Veteran's Guide to Psychedelics

Having walked alongside Kemmi throughout this process, I witnessed her willingness to engage the inner work this path requires with honesty and courage. Her memoir reflects a sincere encounter with the sacrament of Ayahuasca—not as an end in itself, but as a call to listen deeply, remember what matters, and place oneself in service beyond the individual self.

This story is held within community and offered as a gesture of accompaniment for those walking their own paths of spiritual transformation. Sharing this story with the world is an act of responsibility, love, and conscious service.

*-**Inti Munay,** Founder & Director, Centro Espiritualista Luz Do Vegetal Church of Florida*

I've seen how Kemmi's professional life was shaped by duty, impossible choices, and the weight she quietly carried at the end of the day. What she shares in *From the Badge to the Vine* is told with a courage that will disarm even the most skeptical reader—because her honesty isn't performative; it's earned through years of service, responsibility, and hard-won self-reflection. This is a story of healing that feels both credible and deeply human. Her voice lingers long after the final page.

-Lynne A. McDermott, Director of Communications, Harvard Law School

I've served my country and community for more than three decades, and I've known Kemmi Sadler for nearly thirty years. I can say without hesitation that she has earned my deepest respect. This book speaks directly to those who carry the weight of service. Kemmi doesn't romanticize healing, she shows what it actually asks of a life shaped by duty. She's walked through the fire and invites others to take the first step forward, knowing they won't be alone.

-TG Harrell, Assistant Chief of Police, St. Augustine Beach Police Department, St. Augustine Beach, Florida

From the Badge to the Vine by Kemmi Sadler is nothing short of exceptional. If you are a fan of Terrence McKenna, and his search for meaning with the use of entheogens, then you are going to love this memoir. With honesty, humility, and humor, Kemmi teaches us that with a little bit of help we can face long buried truths and find our true self. This book is more than a story about a hallucinogenic experience, it is about courage, discovery, and finding your way back home.

-Shane Dixon, Former Chargé d' Affaires a.i. of the United States in Somalia, U.S. Department of State

I served under Kemmi when she was the Assistant Regional Security Officer supporting the Marine Security Guard program. Through this book, I've come to know the woman behind the badge and recognize how many of our experiences were shared. We all carry the unseen costs of service over the course of a career. Few are willing to examine that cost honestly. She does.

-Migdalia Adair, MSgt, USMC (Ret.)

Kemmi's book is a breathtaking and honest account of the courage and vulnerability needed to face one's demons, an inspiring journey taken on by a woman who has lived and worked in some of the world's most dangerous places. This book is riveting, thought-provoking and will make you ask some tough questions about your inner world. I could not put it down.

-Jeannie Page, Host of The Psychedelic Paradigm Shift.

FROM THE BADGE TO THE VINE

A JOURNEY THROUGH DUTY, TRAUMA, AND HEALING

K.L. SADLER

FROM THE BADGE TO THE VINE

A JOURNEY THROUGH DUTY, TRAUMA, AND HEALING

BY: K.L. SADLER

Edited by Genet Jones / thoughtfulwordsmith.com

Cover Design by Maloka Design Group / v.malokadesign@gmail.com

Published by Legalize The Divine LLC / legalizethedivine.com

Hardcover ISBN: 979-8-9939352-0-1

Paperback ISBN: 979-8-9939352-1-8

Ebook ASIN:

For Dad, who prayed for me every single day.

And for Amel, who walked into the fire for love and never returned.

CONTENTS

FOREWORD

Some stories announce themselves loudly, demanding attention with spectacle and certainty. This is not one of them. *From the Badge to the Vine* moves differently—quietly, deliberately—like a truth long carried that finally consents to be spoken.

I have known Kemmi for much of the life she writes about here, and I can say without hesitation that this book is not an abstraction, nor a retrospective polished by distance. It is the work of someone who has lived fully inside the questions she asks, the losses she names, and the reckonings she refuses to soften. The pages that follow are shaped by experience, not theory—by fire, not commentary.

Kemmi and I share more than a profession. We came from similar beginnings, shaped early by responsibility and resilience, and both carry the quiet weight of a brother lost to heroin—a grief that never truly leaves, only changes form. We learned young that life could fracture without warning, and that survival often requires adaptation long before understanding arrives. Those early lessons echo throughout this book, informing its moral clarity and its refusal to look away.

We also shared a career that demanded everything. As Diplomatic Security Service special agents, we trained together, served together, and endured together—through high-threat environments, through Iraq from 2006 to 2007, and through the crucible of training designed to break you down before the world does. We were captured together during mini-SERE, tested not only for endurance, but for judgment, ethics, and trust under pressure. Those experiences strip pretense quickly. What remains is who you are when comfort, control, and certainty are gone.

Kemmi writes from that place.

The life we chose as DSS agents was meaningful, purposeful, and unsustainable. We ran hard and far, achieved real outcomes, led extraordinary people, and advanced U.S. government objectives in places where failure carried consequences measured in lives. But that pace came at a cost. Alcohol became currency—used to quiet the nervous system, to transition from chaos to stillness, to numb what had no space to be processed in daylight. This book does not sensationalize that reality, nor does it excuse it. Instead, it examines it honestly, with accountability and compassion.

What makes this work exceptional is not simply what Kemmi reveals, but *how* she reveals it. Her ethical struggles are rendered with humility, not self-justification. Her spiritual questions are explored without dogma, fear, or performance. Again and again, she returns to the same central act: recalibrating the compass—relearning how to find true north after years of navigating by mission, rank, and threat matrix.

This is a book about armor—how it protects, how it corrodes, and how difficult it is to set down once it has fused to the body. It is also a book about healing that does not arrive neatly or quickly, but through missteps, courage, and radical honesty. Kemmi does not offer prescriptions. She offers something rarer: lived truth.

You should care about this story because it is not only hers. It belongs to anyone who has given too much of themselves in service of something larger, anyone who has outrun their own reflection, anyone who has sensed—quietly, persistently—that survival is not the same as living. It is a testament to the possibility of reinvention without denial, and to the strength it takes to face one's life without the protection of uniform or role.

Kemmi has written a brave, unsettling, and deeply human book. It is a privilege to stand at its threshold and invite you in.

-Zach Zittle, Retired Supervisory Special Agent, U.S. Department of State, Diplomatic Security Service (DSS Ret.)

PREFACE

I served for over two decades in federal law enforcement and diplomacy, but the views expressed here are mine alone. Any identifying details involving others have been changed or omitted unless I had their permission to share them.

This book is not intended as legal, medical, psychological, or therapeutic advice. If you are navigating health challenges, legal concerns, or spiritual questions, please seek the guidance of qualified professionals you trust. The reflections I share—especially those related to ayahuasca—are not recommendations. They are simply my experience. Like many sacred plants, ayahuasca remains regulated or prohibited in various jurisdictions. It is your responsibility to understand and comply with the laws where you live.

I believe reverence, and respect for lineage, must guide any engagement with sacred plants. Some carry unique cultural and ecological weight, and their survival depends on responsible stewardship. My advocacy for spiritual sovereignty does not mean everything belongs to everyone. Sometimes reverence looks like restraint. Thankfully, the Earth has given us many paths to healing.

If parts of this book make you uncomfortable, I hope you will stay with them. If not, perhaps you will feel called to revisit them. Growth rarely comes without resistance. Know that I have my own discomfort in sharing, but without those parts, my story would not be what it is.

A NOTE ON LANGUAGE

Throughout this book, I refer to Ayahuasca by several names—*Mother Ayahuasca, La Medicina, The Medicine,* and the *Sacrament.*

In traditional settings, *La Medicina* or *The Medicine* is used as a term of reverence, describing the plant's wisdom and capacity to heal the spirit. In more modern church contexts, *Sacrament* is used to honor its sacred purpose and to reflect the evolving language around its ceremonial use.

I use these words interchangeably, but always with the same meaning in mind: not a pharmaceutical, but a sacred plant that is a teacher and a bridge to the Divine.

PART ONE
BENEATH THE BARK

CHAPTER 1
PARTY TRICKS AND PINKY FINGERS

"It is no measure of health to be well adjusted to a profoundly sick society." –Jiddu Krishnamurti

---

Here's a fun fact.

I can stick my entire pinky finger up my left nostril.

A party trick, born of multiple broken noses and a severely deviated septum. Gross, yes—but it was also a surefire way to win a free drink and enough barroom cred to secure my place as "one of the guys." That and an occasional dip of Skoal Wintergreen.

Turns out my collapsed nasal passage was a perfect metaphor for my life: one side wide open, the other closed off. A busted-up breathing system I adapted to over time, without realizing I was suffocating.

That's what everyone does, isn't it? Learn to function with damage. Make it look normal.

Push through. Work harder.

Drink more. Laugh louder.

Make bets at bars and call it toughness, not trauma.

In my defense, I didn't know I wasn't really breathing. I didn't know I wasn't really living. And I didn't know that the thing I feared most—losing control—would be the very thing that saved me.

CHAPTER 2
SNICKERS

"I am not what happened to me. I am what I choose to become."
–Carl Jung

Three days after I was born, my soon-to-be father boarded a plane from St. Louis to pick me up from a hospital in Oregon.

Dad loved to tell the story of my adoption: how he and Mom were at dinner one night when a voice came over the PA system, asking if they were in the restaurant. The caller, a church leader, wanted to know: "Would you like a little girl being born in a few months?"

He'd tell me how people offered to help him on the plane and commented on how well-behaved I was. He'd laugh loudly, as was his way, when he talked about how he came home exhausted, handed me to my mother, and said, "Here, I can't do any more."

Mom wanted to name me Erin Nicole, but Dad had other plans. Without telling her, he wrote "Kemmi Lynn" on every single birth announcement and delivered them to all the mailboxes in their neighborhood. By the time Mom found out, my name was already set in ink.

He'd come up with "Kemmi" because he had served as a Mormon missionary in Japan and had become fond of the name "Kemiko." "Kemmi" was his Americanized version.

Little did he know that the gift of a unique name would translate to the gift of being comfortable in my skin from a very early age. When I'd do something others found unusual (a.k.a. quirky or crazy), I'd say, "Well, I'm an original." The proof? I never, not once, found my name on a keychain or magnet in a souvenir shop.

After finishing dental school, dad set up his practice in the oldest town west of the Mississippi: Sainte Geneviève, Missouri.

I was a carefree kid, always giggling. Dad told me once that even in my sleep, he'd catch me snickering. So, naturally, he started calling me "Snickers."

When I was three years old, my parents got a call inviting them to meet a five-year old boy, Rees, who'd been placed into foster care. Over lunch the social worker asked them, "So, what do you think? Do you want to take him home?"

After collecting his belongings—a puppy-print blanket, pajamas, and a bottle of asthma medicine—we were on the way home.

Dad told me that later that night he found me "showing Rees the ropes." I had taken on the role of big sister, despite being two years his junior.

A few years later, a six-month-old boy, Spencer, arrived. My first memory of him is Mom changing his diaper on the living room couch and him peeing on her. I thought it was the funniest thing I'd ever seen.

We grew up in a wooded subdivision a few miles outside of town. Our house backed up to a lake. There were more wooded lots than houses, and we built clubhouses, caught crawdads, played in the dirt, and explored the woods.

It was the era of MTV, but we didn't have cable, so we made up our own entertainment. We invented games like "bike tag," which involved yanking the bike out from under the rider as they rode through a gauntlet of outstretched grabbing hands. This led to one of two broken noses I suffered early in life. The other occurred when I was walking around with my eyes closed, slipped on a slice of zucchini, and slid headfirst into the stove.

Eventually I met both of my biological parents, and learned that I was the unexpected result of a short-lived relationship that began in a tennis class at BYU. (Funny, I didn't realize tennis was a contact sport.) It was an odd revelation—equal parts amusing and surreal. In the end, I saw it for what it was: a twist of fate that set my life in motion.

Throughout my life, people often asked, "When did you find out you were adopted?" There was no single moment; I always knew. It was never a secret. The first time it ever occurred to me that there was something defective about being adopted was in elementary school. I can still picture the bus I was on, and the girl who told me, "You don't have a real family. Your real family didn't want you."

I hadn't realized I was different until that moment. Her words hit like a slap, sharp and disorienting. I didn't tell anyone. I swallowed it and moved on, the way kids do. Just tucked that moment away deep inside, where it quietly shaped the way I saw myself for years to come. I became full of questions—not the casual curiosity of a child, but a restless, persistent need to understand.

Why had I been given away? What had I done—or not done—that made my biological mother decide she didn't want me? Did she ever think about me? Who was my birth father? Would I ever get to know the truth?

I probably didn't have those words at the time, but the emotions and yearning were already taking root.

I was in high school when I first spoke to my biological mother on the phone. The first words out of her mouth were, "I'm glad I decided not to have an abortion."

My mind scrambled to process what she had said. There was no malice in her tone, just a simple statement of fact. I wasn't sure what I was supposed to say to that—my very existence, reduced to a choice that had almost gone the other way.

"Um... Me too...?" I finally said.

I struggled to connect with my adoptive mother. There was an emotional distance between us. I wanted to feel chosen. Instead, I sometimes felt—I guess you could say "placed." Loved, but not known. Welcomed, but not quite understood.

I'd look up at the moon in the night sky and sing, "Somewhere out there, beneath the pale moonlight," and let myself believe that my "real" family was out there wondering about me. Maybe even missing me.

Writing this now, I wonder if that's where it started—my need to understand the story beneath the surface, the parts no one talks about.

CHAPTER 3
HARD WORK U

"Opportunities are usually disguised as hard work, so most people don't recognize them." –Ann Landers

By the time I graduated high school in 1991, I felt suffocated at home and saw college as an out. Mom and I were both strong-willed and stubborn. At eighteen, I couldn't see that our butting heads came from being alike. All I knew was that I needed space.

I had kept my grades decent, but not outstanding enough for scholarships. I ran track, also not well enough for scholarships, despite breaking the record in the 1600-meter. I ran because it gave me an outlet that nothing else did: a temporary escape from everything that weighed me down.

I applied to the University of Missouri and was accepted, but when my parents asked me how I planned to pay for it, I was hit with a jolt of panic. I had simply assumed they planned to pay for college, but that was not the case, so Mizzou was not a viable option—or at least not an affordable one.

One day in the counseling office, the counselor saw my desperation and handed me a brochure for The College of the Ozarks (CofO)—also known as "Hard Work U." It was a private Christian college. It boasted a work-study program that helped students earn a bachelor's degree without taking out any loans. I applied and was grateful to be accepted.

I didn't choose to attend CofO because it was a Christian school. I went because it was a way to get a degree without debt, which I knew would change the trajectory of my life.

I was not afraid of hard work. I had been working for my dad since I was twelve or so, first cleaning the dental office, and later taking patient X-rays and polishing teeth.

Fifteen hours a week on campus and two forty-hour workweeks per semester for 100% of tuition was a trade I was willing to make. If I worked an additional twelve forty-hour weeks over the summers, that covered housing costs. I'd graduate with zero debt—a deal too good to pass up.

My campus jobs included the Ralph Foster Museum, the landscaping department, and eventually campus security, but sadly resulted in no walking-around money. So I also found work off-campus waiting tables at Uncle Joe's Bar-B-Q, and fell in love with BBQ as well as the couple who owned the restaurant. They became like surrogate parents.

I also worked at "The Track" running go-karts. "Gas is on the right, brake is on the left, do not bump, swerve, or force anyone into the rail. When the light comes on at the bottom of the hill, return to the pit and remain seated." I don't know how many times I repeated that phrase over the PA, but it is forever ingrained in my brain.

With all that work, you might think I didn't have time for fun.

You'd be wrong.

The minute I was on my own and free to make my own rules, I went a tad wild. At the very first party I went to with my roommate, everyone at the party was drinking beer, which I had not yet acquired a taste for. Someone offered me a bottle of Mad Dog 20/20 from the back of the fridge instead. It had around three fingers of purple liquid left in the bottle.

I drank it. And passed out on the couch.

A new nickname was born. From that night on, every time I arrived at The Track and the host of that party was working, he'd get on the PA and broadcast, "MAD DOG!"

He was poking fun, but I didn't mind it. I felt like one of the party crowd. It felt good to belong.

I spent the first two years at CofO partying, and the next two years desperately trying to recover my GPA. I continued the pattern of over-serving myself early in the evening. My roommate, Mindy, would load me into her Mustang 5.0 and haul me back to the dorm, then resume her night out. One night I guess I was coherent enough to resist being cut off, but not enough to stay on my feet. I made it as far as the hallway before passing out on the floor. After being discovered drunk on campus, and not the first time, I was placed on dorm probation. So, my junior year I moved off campus. Problem solved.

I wanted to follow in my dad's footsteps of being in a profession that helped people. I had watched him take things on trade for dental work from people who could not afford to pay. I had gone to the office with him in the middle of the night many times, to assist with patients in pain too severe to wait for office hours.

Though Dad had hoped I'd consider dentistry, my up-close-and-personal exposure to the field never sparked a real interest. I tried volunteering at the local hospital as a candy striper (although because of a misprint on the name tags, I was officially a "candy stripper").

Turned out, neither of those career paths were for me. The smells, the bedpans, the confinement of being inside were enough to dissuade me.

One day, my dad asked, "Have you ever thought about going into law enforcement?"

The moment he said it, something clicked.

I remember thinking that by being a police officer, I could help people *before* they ended up in the hospital. I could also stand up to bullies. Maybe being a cop would allow me to do some good in the world.

I declared Criminal Justice as my major.

In the end, I walked away with a degree, a deep appreciation for hard work, and the knowledge that I could carve my path—even within a system that didn't quite fit me.

CHAPTER 4
THE QUESTION OF GOD

"The truth is not always in the hands of those who claim to know it. It waits for the seeker, in silence, in stillness, in the spaces between words." –Unknown

Being a private Christian college, CofO had a requirement to attend a certain number of non-denominational church services each semester. If I recall correctly, it was around six Sunday services, plus a couple of guest speakers or performers. I met the requirement, but beyond that, I had no interest in church. In fact, I despised it. To me, organized religion felt sexist, oppressive, suffocating, and judgmental. I had been raised in a Mormon household, and church for three hours every Sunday, plus church activities on Wednesday night, had never been optional.

I also resented the routine interviews with Mormon church leadership, where I was expected to list out all my sins in a private meeting with the bishop. As a teenage girl, sitting face-to-face with a middle-aged man and discussing my "sins" and my dating life felt deeply invasive. Even now, the memory makes my skin crawl.

So as I left for college, I also walked away from Mormonism, but not without a heavy dose of guilt that I carried for years. If you're familiar with the term "Catholic guilt," I'd argue that Mormon guilt is just as heavy. I often felt that I was "bad" for not going to church. According to what I'd been taught, I was most likely bound for hell for ignoring what I "knew" to be true.

Walking away also left a vacuum I didn't know how to fill. I still believed in something, but I didn't know how to name it—or trust it. I didn't realize that faith and organized religion weren't the same thing, or that spirituality could exist outside of dogma.

I realized eventually that the seed of spirituality in my life wasn't planted in a church building. It came from my dad. Dad wasn't preachy. He didn't quote scripture or talk about hell. He was simply deeply intuitive. He understood people, even when they were making mistakes—or maybe especially then. He moved through life with a quiet wisdom that stuck with me long after I'd turned my back on organized religion.

As a church leader, he was a lot of things to a lot of people. Brother Sadler, Bishop Sadler, Elder Sadler. Outside the church, he was also Doctor Sadler and Mr. Sadler. He said that when I was little I asked him if it was okay if I just called him Dad.

Once, after helping someone through the loss of a loved one, he told me he had felt a spirit hug him. Not metaphorically; literally. A spirit had wrapped its arms around him in thanks. He said it so plainly: a statement of fact, with no explanations or proof needed.

It was the first time I considered that the spiritual world might be real, even if I didn't understand it and wanted nothing to do with the institutions that claimed to own it.

My skepticism toward organized religion deepened during my sophomore year of college, when I tried to find my birth father. I had barely enough information from my birth mother to make the search possible. I found a company that offered a unique service: if they could locate the person, they would deliver a letter to them from you, with your contact information. It was up to the person being sought whether they responded.

Some months later, a letter arrived. I wasn't sure what I had hoped for. Connection? Closure? Answers?

The response stirred up more than I expected. My reaching out had created a ripple effect—forcing a conversation between my birth father and his children. I hadn't meant to disrupt anything, but I couldn't un-ring the bell.

The letter explained that he had been excommunicated from the Mormon church over me. My conception—my existence—had cost him something he valued deeply. He eventually earned his way back into the fold, but that knowledge hardened something in me. If that was how "God's church" handled complexity—by casting people out instead of helping and welcoming them—I wanted no part of it.

I tucked the letter away with another I had found, this one from my birth mother to my adoptive parents. In it, she wrote of the great sacrifice it had been to give me up, and how she had chosen them after much prayer. She believed she was doing the right thing. All she asked in return was both simple, and everything:

1. That they love me, no matter what I did.

2. That they remind me I was good, even when I made mistakes.

3. That they teach me that, even if I did bad things, I was still a child of God.

For the next thirty years, I wasn't sure where I stood on the question of God. I believed in a higher power, but I struggled to define my beliefs.

Instead of aligning with a single faith, I became fascinated by ancient religions and sacred sites, drawn to the origins of spiritual traditions across cultures. I visited sacred sites across continents whenever the opportunity arose—Jerusalem, the Great Pyramids, Stonehenge, Petra, Chichén Itzá, Teotihuacán, and others.

In 2004, I had the unique opportunity to visit Bamiyan, Afghanistan, once home to two towering Buddha statues carved into the cliffs in the sixth century and destroyed by the Taliban in 2001. Climbing the spiral staircases carved into the rock, standing where the Buddhas' heads had once gazed out over the valley, remains one of the most sacred moments of my life—a quiet intersection of history, grief, and awe. There was a peace in that ancient space, a stark juxtaposition to the violence and intolerance that had tried to erase it.

I wanted to know what faith looked like before institutions, priests, bishops, and all the pomp and circumstance. I could not shake the feeling that these "middlemen" served as barriers to direct communication with God. Ancient traditions emphasizing direct connection with the divine resonated with me deeply.

I once found myself in Jerusalem, standing inside the Church of the Holy Sepulchre. I was struck by the fact that three of the world's major religions trace their origins to that tiny city. Outside, at the Wailing Wall, devout worshippers pressed their foreheads to the ancient stones, slipping handwritten prayers into the cracks. The call to prayer rang out from a mosque on the Temple Mount, its melodic echo weaving through the narrow streets like a thread of devotion.

I was wearing a Buddhist bracelet, a necklace with a Mayan sun and moon, earrings that bore the Celtic triskele, and had an aging tattoo of an ankh on my back—all ancient symbols I had been drawn to in my search for meaning.

I watched the faithful kneel at the place where Jesus is said to have been laid after the crucifixion, and thought about the bloodshed and conflict surrounding the belief that only one version of God is correct.

Despite my distaste for religion, I was grateful for my Mormon upbringing and all that it had provided me, especially my sense of right and wrong. I didn't need the buildings and the chain of command to know what was right. Or, more importantly, to do what was right.

For over thirty years, if anyone had asked about my faith, I would have given the same answer as millions of others: "I'm spiritual but not religious." I hadn't rejected faith itself, only the structures that tried to contain it. I hadn't turned away from the divine; I was searching for a way to connect with it on my own terms.

CHAPTER 5
AWOL

In the summer of 1993, CofO added an ROTC program to its curriculum, offering six credit hours plus a semester of lodging for attending a six-week ROTC boot camp at Fort Knox, Kentucky. No strings attached.

I signed up, excelled at the boot camp, and was offered a slot in Airborne School at Fort Benning, Georgia. I arrived with the best of intentions, but I didn't complete the course. To this day, it may be the only thing I've ever started and not finished—aside from a brief attempt to take up golf at age fifty.

The short version of this story is that I went "AWOL" (fortunately for my record, I was on a trial basis with no formal enlistment obligation) from Airborne School that summer, to return to Fort Knox with an ROTC drill sergeant. I had fallen for him and spent the rest of the summer hiding out in his barracks, trying not to be seen by his chain of command while driving around base in his very recognizable jacked-up Toyota truck.

There is probably a good reason that dating and marrying an ROTC cadet is frowned upon. In hindsight, we may not have been the best influences on each other.

The drill sergeant wasn't the only reason I didn't want to stay at Airborne School. I didn't like anyone telling me what to do, which made the military a spectacularly bad fit for me.

And perhaps my biggest concern was my recurring breathing issues. During high school, I'd had corrective nasal surgery to remove scar tissue that had covered my airway thanks to my second broken nose. The blockage had made it difficult to breathe freely while running track, often leaving me feeling that I was on the verge of hyperventilating.

It had been several years since the surgery, but I wondered if the scar tissue had returned. I found it difficult to breathe deeply and was often short of breath. It was getting annoying that every time I embarked on a new chapter of my life, my breathing issues ramped up.

I was worried Georgia's heat and humidity would exacerbate it. I was also probably a bit terrified at the thought of jumping out of a plane. So, running off with a man fifteen years my senior seemed like a better idea.

I used to think that I left Airborne School because I was afraid—of the heat, of the jumps, of failure. I'm sure all of that was true, but it wasn't the whole story.

Looking back, I see that my resistance to structure wasn't rebellion, it was a compass. That compass guided me away from paths that weren't meant for me, even though I didn't yet know the path that was meant for me.

Walking away from ROTC may have been the first time I chose the unknown over the expected route. I didn't have the language for it, but I knew something didn't feel right. Sometimes, going AWOL is how we find ourselves.

If I'd only listened to my inner compass about the drill sergeant as well, I'd have avoided some heartache along the way. But that's not always how we learn, is it?

CHAPTER 6
SAPD

"Courage is not the absence of fear, but rather the judgment that something else is more important than fear." –Ambrose Redmoon

---

A year later, in December 1994, I graduated from college, married the drill sergeant, and returned to Fort Knox. This time, I didn't have to sneak around on base.

I began selling Kirby vacuum cleaners door to door for a few months while we prepared to move north for his next posting at Fort Richardson, Alaska.

In Alaska, I worked at a homeless shelter for teenagers, a drug and alcohol rehab center, and a halfway house. My breathing issues continued. I eventually sought treatment and was diagnosed with a deviated septum and collapsed nasal passage on one side. Once again, I underwent surgery.

I loved being surrounded by wild and untamed nature, and witnessing the quiet power of landscapes untouched by human hands. One winter morning my headlights cut through the darkness and illuminated the air ahead of me, glittering with frozen particles. I'd never seen ice fog before, and it was like driving inside a snow globe. I didn't need religion to feel that this was a sacred moment. It reminded me that magic existed, even in the bitter cold of an Alaskan winter.

Following a partial malfunction with his parachute, the drill sergeant was medically discharged from the Army. He survived, but lived with chronic pain. Alaska had given us a lot, but after the long winters, isolation, and his injury, we craved warmth, sunlight, and a fresh start. So we packed up and headed south to the Sunshine State.

Before deciding where in Florida we wanted to settle, we spent some time in Tampa with my husband's family. I once again sought medical help for the recurring sensation of not being able to breathe. It wasn't constant, but it would hit in waves: tightness in my chest, and a sense that no matter how deeply I inhaled, I wasn't getting enough oxygen.

The doctors hooked me up to machines, ran pulmonary function tests, did blood-work, and took x-rays. The results came back: no signs of asthma, physical abnormalities, or any other obvious diagnosis. Yet I still couldn't breathe.

Eventually, they gave it a name: stress-induced asthma. It was a way of saying: we can't find anything wrong with your lungs, but your body seems to think otherwise.

That completely unsettled me. It meant I might never fully understand what was happening inside me. It also implied it was all in my head, which made me feel defective. I had no idea that these symptoms were part of a low hum of panic. My lungs were responding to unseen tensions that my conscious mind was carefully avoiding.

A few weeks later, we drove up the Eastern seaboard, starting in Sarasota and ending in Jacksonville. While exploring St. Augustine, I noticed a local classified listing for 911 dispatchers. It must be a sign, I thought. St. Augustine, the nation's oldest city, seemed the perfect complement to Ste. Geneviève, the town where I'd grown up and the oldest town west of the Mississippi.

I applied, got the job, and began working full time as a 911 operator. Florida required police officers to complete the police academy and receive a state certification, so I attended the police academy while I worked as a 911 operator. I put in 80-hour weeks for six months, running on sheer willpower, caffeine, and the occasional power nap.

My immune system gave out about five months in, and I came down with a high fever and a nasty case of bronchitis. Back then, the expectation was to power through. No one stayed home for a fever or exhaustion. Or at least, I didn't. I sat in the back of the classroom, half-delirious, trying to take notes while practically marinating in cough syrup.

I lived about thirty minutes from town and had an hour's commute each day. One night, I blinked and suddenly found myself parked in the driveway—engine running, headlights still on. I had no memory of the drive home or shifting into park. I had been there for several hours, too exhausted to make it inside my house.

When I graduated from the academy, I slept for over twenty-four hours straight. The only reason I made it through those six months was because a dear friend and colleague let me take naps behind the counter —out of sight to anyone entering Dispatch—on slow nights.

Occasionally, I'd wake up, and an officer would be in dispatch chatting with my friend, telling her their deepest and darkest secrets. I'd lie quietly, waiting for them to leave. Thankfully, any secrets I overheard have long since been forgotten.

After finishing the academy in 1998, I started on patrol for the St. Augustine Police Department (SAPD).

When I interviewed for the job, I was asked why I wanted to join the police force.

When I was growing up in Ste. Geneviève, people often let their dogs run free. That was true for our collie, Patches, and later for Teddy, a small mixed-breed.

When I was twelve, our neighbor shot Teddy for "trespassing." I found her at the top of our driveway, bleeding from her neck. She was harmless; he was cruel. He was also big and scary. But that didn't stop me from standing across the street, in my best friend's driveway, pointing my finger at him and giving him a piece of my mind.

I reported him to the police, believing justice would be served. Turned out, he was the police, so nothing happened. So I made signs to put around the neighborhood informing people that the man who lived at (insert address) shot dogs. Thankfully, Teddy survived, but the wound left lasting damage that shortened her life.

In my interview to become a cop, I recall saying that I wanted to be a force for good, to help balance the scales. If there were "bad cops" out there, then I wanted to be a "good cop."

I loved being a cop. Everything about it: the uniform, the patrol car, the rush of a car chase, the people I worked with. Especially the people I worked with. There was a professional camaraderie I'd never experienced before.

Most of all, I loved being able to help people. I prided myself on using officer discretion: focusing on the intent of the law rather than rigidly enforcing the letter. Common sense dictated when an arrest was necessary and when a warning was the better course.

I gave a lot of breaks to young people. I had a close call with a DUI while attending CofO that scared me straight. A security officer who worked at The Track—a friend—was also a reserve deputy. He was in the car when I got pulled over one fateful night, and convinced the deputy I was a good kid—even though I was being belligerent. A DUI that night would have drastically changed the course of my life. I never forgot that and tried to pay it forward.

Crack cocaine was a big problem in the late 90's, as I was learning the ropes. The first time I found a crack rock during a vehicle search, my field training officer said, "Are you sure it's not a French fry crumb?" I tested it. It was not.

I took a training on meth labs, which were expected to be the next craze. I began pulling trash, looking for signs that crack or meth was being cooked in the residence. I stealthily loaded trash bags from the side of the road into the trunk of my Crown Victoria and brought them to the station. From there, I'd spread them out in the vehicle bay looking for clues. That is, until the detective sergeant yelled at me for "doing detective work."

Tail between my legs, I went back to traffic stops and responding to calls in my zone. I figured the best way to get back at him was to do only what I was asked, and nothing more.

A short time later, I volunteered for a detail at Flagler College, which was comparatively low-key. I was pursuing a master's in public administration at the University of North Florida in Jacksonville, so working on the college detail allowed me to work around my class schedule. It also gave me access to the campus library for research, a definite perk.

I enjoyed responding to calls on campus, chatting with the Flagler College security officers—most of whom were retired NYPD officers— and interacting with the students, who began calling me Officer Kem.

Taking graduate classes in the evenings and working full-time was demanding. Still, I grew frustrated with the lack of opportunities for extra income in the form of off-duty jobs. I was also discouraged when my proposal to move to twelve-hour shifts was struck down, despite the chief's initial support. Two holdouts had killed it.

So, as much as I loved being at SAPD, I eventually accepted that passion alone wouldn't be enough. If I wanted more, I had to look elsewhere.

My time at SAPD laid the foundation for everything that came after. I became adept at exercising authority without being demanding, developed a calm presence in chaotic environs, and learned to adapt quickly in unfamiliar situations.

As a federal agent working in foreign lands, war zones, and high-stakes environments, I was often praised for my poise under pressure. I credit that steadiness to my days on the streets of St. Augustine.

CHAPTER 7
GREENER PASTURES

"Sometimes you have to let go of the life you planned to find the life that's waiting for you." –Joseph Campbell

---

On September 10, 2001, I turned in my badge at SAPD. I had accepted a contract with Combat Support Associates (CSA), a Department of Defense contractor tasked with base security for Camp Doha in Kuwait.

The next morning, I packed up my house and loaded my life into a storage unit, unaware that the America I knew was changing forever on live television.

Most of the furniture was already packed, so my phone sat on the kitchen floor. It started ringing with concerned friends and family who wanted to know if I still planned to take the job in the Middle East. After the first call, I plugged the TV into the wall, and sat down in front of it on the living room floor as the second plane slammed into the towers.

A few minutes later, the police chief called to offer me my job back. I appreciated the offer, but I had given my word. In the wake of everything, backing out didn't just feel like breaking a contract—it seemed unpatriotic.

Even though I had walked away from my chance to join the military, I remained deeply loyal to my country, and by extension, to the institutions that represented it. I was still too young and naive to realize that true patriotism is not blind allegiance, it is holding your country to its ideals.

Even knowing what I know now, I still would have gone to Kuwait. I just would have understood that fighting for freedom and fighting for policy aren't always the same thing.

When I arrived in Kuwait, only a handful of those set to begin the September orientation class had arrived. Presumably, they had broken their contracts out of fear.

Those first few days and weeks were intense. My only international travel had been trips to Canada and the Bahamas. Adjusting to life in Kuwait was an entirely new experience. The desert heat, cultural differences, and the looks I received for not wearing local garb were like stepping into another world.

One evening, I went looking for a grocery store near my apartment. It should have been a simple errand, but I got completely lost. I didn't have a local cell phone yet, and GPS apps were still a few years away.

As I wandered, the reality of my situation sank in. My heart pounded as I walked faster. It was beginning to get dark, and I was drawing unwanted looks as I walked alone through unfamiliar streets.

I spotted a man sitting outside an apartment building. He was British, drinking a beer. My first thought was, "How did he manage to get beer in a country where alcohol is illegal?" (A question I'd soon answer for myself: know the right people and be willing to pay $150 for a $20 bottle of Jack.)

My second thought was, "Oh, thank God, someone I can ask for help."

He suggested that the taxi drivers would know where CSA had their apartments, and walked with me to the nearest taxi stand. I was only about a block from where I needed to be and made it home safely. In a new and visceral way, I understood the need to be aware of my surroundings.

I also began to seriously reconsider my marriage. Going to Kuwait had been a way to get out of debt and have a clean break. We had both signed contracts with CSA and were sharing an apartment. We were working sixty hours a week or more, exhausted, and not getting along. The tension between us was so intense my breathing started to deteriorate again.

At night, I'd lie awake with a tightness in my chest. During the day, I felt short of breath. At first, I blamed the desert heat. I distracted myself with work, not a difficult task considering that I was working twelve-hour days for weeks on end without a day off. But something deeper kept stirring.

I started to ask bigger questions. I'd gone to college because I wanted to leave home. Then I'd become a cop because I thought I needed a purpose. When I'd reached that goal, I went to graduate school because I thought I needed more knowledge. When that wasn't enough, I took a job in Kuwait because I had decided I needed to see the world and experience other cultures.

But here I was, living out those decisions, not necessarily even regretting them, but still feeling a longing for fulfillment elsewhere. Something was missing.

I began to wonder: *Is it God that I'm missing?*

One day, I surprised even myself and went to a Mormon church service on base. The drill sergeant told me it scared him that I was going to church.

That moment helped solidify my decision. I would not stay in a relationship where my significant other was afraid of my search for fulfillment and personal growth. I would file for divorce, leave Kuwait, and begin a new chapter of my life.

It was in the middle of these long, grinding weeks that I first learned about the U.S. Department of State's Diplomatic Security Service (DSS). One afternoon, a colleague who routinely attended security briefings at the U.S. Embassy told me about this little-known law enforcement agency. "It's the best-kept secret in federal law enforcement," he told me.

I looked into it. DSS investigated passport and visa fraud (especially relevant given the events of September 11th), protected foreign dignitaries and the U.S. Secretary of State, and traveled the world overseeing security operations at U.S. embassies. I was hooked. The position was open, and it felt like a sign. I scrambled to get my application in by the deadline, and within a few months I had a job offer.

Kuwait had served its purpose, but it wasn't something I could have done very long. In one two-week pay period I logged 173 hours. The hardest part of the job was simply staying awake.

There were also too many things that didn't make sense.

Each day, we were issued three fifteen-round 9mm magazines and told to load them with ten rounds each. I loaded two of them to full capacity and left one empty.

When a supervisor told me I was doing it wrong, I asked, "If I need them, wouldn't it be better to reload once instead of twice?" The look on his face made it clear that critical thinking by subordinates was not appreciated.

Then there were the helmets. My scrawny neck wasn't strong enough to carry around those 4.2 pounds of Kevlar for extended periods of time. I started getting awful headaches, and an X-ray confirmed I had compressed vertebrae.

I called in a favor from a friend back home. A week later, I had a plastic replica helmet. I gave it a good scuffing to make it look like it had seen some things, climbed into the Humvee turret, parked myself behind the .50-caliber machine gun, turned my head from side to side, and grinned like a kid who'd just gotten away with something.

Leaving Kuwait was a bittersweet goodbye. Despite the heat, the headaches, and the endless twelve-hour shifts, Kuwait had given me more than a paycheck and a new stamp in my passport.

One night around 3:00 a.m., I found myself sprawled on top of a Humvee, in the middle of the desert, watching a meteor shower and marveling at how familiar the sky was despite being so far from home.

I had come mostly for the money, sure—a way out of debt and a failing marriage—but what I found was a little window into another world. Not to mention the change in perspective that comes from living somewhere completely unfamiliar, and realizing you can't outrun yourself.

CHAPTER 8

THE MIDDLE GROUND

"Sometimes, you find yourself in the middle of nowhere, and sometimes, in the middle of nowhere, you find yourself." – Unknown

I left the desert heat and returned to the U.S. in 2003, with a few months of breathing room before I would begin the Basic Special Agent Course (BSAC) at the Federal Law Enforcement Training Center (FLETC) in Glynco, Georgia.

I spent a few weeks out West and then went to the Ozarks to see a dear friend whose property sat high on a remote mountainside. We were sitting on her porch, taking in the view across the valley, when I remarked, "It's so peaceful here."

She replied, "You know, the property that borders us is for sale. We could take the horses up there and check it out."

A few minutes later, the horses crested the hill into a clearing overgrown with scrub oak and kudzu. But in my mind's eye, I saw its potential.

In the center of the neglected field stood a large, dead oak tree. At the top of the oak appeared to be a large, white owl.

I did a double take and nudged my horse closer. To my disappointment, it was only a branch, twisted and broken, its pale wood in stark contrast to the rest of the tree. Still, something about it wouldn't let me go. It had looked like an owl—a guardian. Even knowing it was only a branch, it felt like something more.

I had always been drawn to twisted trees. The more deformed, bent by the weather, growing out of rocks or places where they shouldn't have survived, the more they spoke to me, like they were defying the odds and refusing to take no for an answer.

The lyrics of my favorite song, "The Middle Ground," rushed into my head. I had first heard it live at a small venue in St. Louis with a friend who was a 70's music fanatic. As I sat on my horse in the middle of that scrubby field, I heard Rik Emmet's voice:

Last night I dreamed of a long-forgotten place

High upon a hill with the cool wind in my face

And the air was clean and clear, and I could see for miles around

And in my heart, I knew I had come home

And in my soul, there was a peace I'd never known

And so, I laid my claim to this sacred place I'd found

And I stand the middle ground.

I swallowed hard, my chest tightening. I was meant to own this land. I had never been so sure of anything in my life.

I was recently divorced, and technically I was unemployed. I had my conditional employment letter, but doubted I'd be able to get a loan. I went for it anyway. To my great surprise and relief, I was approved and became the proud owner of a remote piece of land in the Ozark Mountains. I named it The Middle Ground.

I cleared a spot, camped on it, and got to know the land as I worked. I dreamed of building a house—a place where I could return between assignments and on vacations, and eventually retire.

I quickly realized the land was so remote that it would be impossible, or at least cost-prohibitive, to connect to the power grid. I accepted the challenge and bought books on alternative energy and passive solar design. I drew plans on graph paper, designing and redesigning the layout again and again until I had a design I couldn't improve upon.

In 2009, after being away from home for sixteen years, I took a position at the Resident Office in St. Louis, Missouri. My father's health was declining. He'd had a quadruple bypass while I was in Kuwait in 2003, and had become diabetic in the years since. I couldn't shake the pull to be closer to home.

Plus, I'd be within five hours of The Middle Ground—close enough to oversee construction on the weekends. And if the world ever fell apart, I'd have a place to go.

My DSS friends came to call the property "The Compound." But to me, it was my sanctuary, my escape from everyone and everything. The place I could always return to, no matter how far I wandered.

PART TWO
SCORCHED EARTH, SACRED GROUND

CHAPTER 9

TWENTY YEARS A DIPLOMAT WITH A GUN

"Sometimes you don't realize the weight of something you've been carrying until you feel the weight of its release." –Unknown

---

The next twenty years, from January of 2004 through April of 2024, went by in a flash. Those twenty years were defined by incredible moments—some surreal, some terrifying, some comical, and others that still make me shake my head in disbelief. Sometimes I would think, *I can't believe I get paid to do this.*

One of my first temporary duty details was to the Winter Olympics in Torino, Italy. My team was tasked with working the opening and closing ceremonies and all of the medals ceremonies. At the opening ceremony, I was standing on the floor when the Olympic flame was carried out to light the torch. I looked over, and there it was, not two feet away from me. A few days later, an athlete who'd won a gold and silver asked me to hold the medals while he used the restroom.

Sometimes, I had a front row seat to history. While serving in Iraq in 2006, I had the opportunity to attend Saddam Hussein's trial for a day.

From a balcony above the courtroom, I watched and listened through translation headphones as Saddam sat seemingly undisturbed by the horrific testimonies of Kurdish citizens who had been subjected to his chemical attacks.

The job also gave me access to incredible cultural experiences. My gardener in Uganda once invited me to his village to go pig hunting with handmade spears. The few pigs we saw escaped our human fence-line masterfully. It was an exhilarating experience, though I'm grateful it was an unsuccessful one.

In Ankara, Turkey, while on a protection detail for Secretary of State Condoleezza Rice, a group of agents went carpet shopping. We bonded with the shop owners and were soon enjoying a four-course meal in the middle of the store. I treasure the memory of breaking bread while surrounded by beautiful handmade carpets.

I once "had" to learn to ski—in case the ambassador we were protecting hit the slopes while in Aspen, Colorado. I had never been on skis, but I took to it naturally and loved it.

Of course, it wasn't always sunshine and rainbows.

CHAPTER 10

CLOSE CALLS AND HARD GOODBYES

"Grief is the price we pay for love." –Queen Elizabeth II

For all the highs, there were also the gut-wrenching lows, moments of sheer terror, and unspeakable heartbreak.

Once, I was in a remote area of El Salvador with my FSNI (Foreign Service National Investigator, the DSS term for local citizens who assisted in our work). We were only tracking down a passport-fraud suspect, but it didn't take long to realize we weren't in friendly territory.

As we made our way back to the main road, we discovered a barricade of trees, deliberately placed, blocking the narrow, one-lane road that had brought us this way not twenty minutes before. There was no way around. We would have to clear the road, and the situation had all the hallmarks of an ambush.

I jumped out, quickly dragging the trees out of the road with one hand as I scanned the tree line, my other hand ready to draw my weapon. My FSNI inched the vehicle forward as I cleared the road.

I used to tease him about his slow and cautious driving habits. Not that time. He hit the gas full throttle as soon as I jumped in, and got us out of there in a hurry. We laughed about it later—much later.

Another time, "mistakes were made" and I got bad directions driving from El Salvador to Ruinas de Copan in Honduras. What should have been a three-hour trip turned into six hours on nearly impassable roads through the mountains, in torrential rains, at night. I had to slow down for massive speed bumps in each town. Young men stood nearby, looking menacing.

Honduras was neck-and-neck with El Salvador as the murder capital of the world. Rampant gang violence spanned both countries. When we stopped for directions we were literally told, "you can't get there from here." For some inexplicable reason we pressed on anyway. I was pretty sure we were about to become a cautionary tale, and I have never been so relieved to reach a destination unharmed in my life.

Perhaps my dumbest move was during a six-week assignment to Iraq in 2004. I hopped a flight with a buddy from college who was flying Black Hawks for the Army and had invited me to tag along on a trip to Tikrit and Mosul.

Telling no one in my chain of command, I showed up at the LZ (landing zone) and went for a joyride. Um, I mean an Iraq orientation flight.

The journey was surreal. People were farming, dogs chased us as we flew overhead, kids were playing. It looked like normalcy, not life impacted by war.

My daydreaming was interrupted by the gunner's voice in my headphones: "They're firing on us." I barely had time to see the blue car sitting on the side of the road below before we tilted hard as the gunner returned fire. Within seconds, the threat was behind us.

Iraq at the time was the Wild West. Anyone could show up at an LZ and hop on a helicopter, no paperwork or authorizations needed. Still, leaving for a day trip with no official reason to be out and about was not the brightest idea I ever had. I had been on the job for all of three months, which is apparently about how long it takes to develop just enough confidence to do something really dumb.

That time, the only thing on the line was my own safety. Other times, that was not the case.

When the disastrous withdrawal from Afghanistan unraveled in 2021, the Embassy told our Afghan staff to go home and wait for instructions. When instructions did not come, they reached out to former supervisors, desperate for guidance. I had departed my assignment in Afghanistan only two years prior, so I was one of those supervisors.

My team and I spent several sleepless nights on WhatsApp, coordinating with our Afghan staff and trying to get information pushed out to them. I reached out to colleagues, trying to confirm if there were evacuation plans, and trying to understand why there was no communication taking place. It soon became clear that my inquiries were not welcome. From my colleagues' frustration, I sensed that their hands were tied.

I also knew we owed our local staff more. Their lives were on the line. They had been told to go home and wait for instruction, and they had done so, while thousands of others had stormed the airport, many successfully boarding flights.

One of the FSNIs sent me a picture of herself in a yellow scarf, with a message that read, "The Taliban are searching for me by name. I cannot wait any longer. Please tell them I'm on my way to the airport."

I forwarded the photo to a DSS agent I knew at HKIA (Hamid Karzai International Airport). He sent one of himself, so she'd know who to look for, standing on top of the concrete barricades that surrounded HKIA. Somehow, he spotted her in the massive crowd outside the heavily guarded gate.

The updates via WhatsApp came excruciatingly slowly. My heart sank when I read, "The military has closed the gate. No one else is getting in."

A few moments later, she sent, "I'm inside." She was safe.

Not every story had the same happy ending, but that deserves its own chapter.

By the time I turned in my "creds" in 2024, I had protected four of the six officials who had been U.S. Secretaries of State during my tenure, been in the presence of two U.S. presidents, provided security for countless foreign dignitaries including the Dalai Lama, and traveled to forty countries, setting foot on six continents in the process.

But beyond the adrenaline, chaos, heartbreak, and history I had witnessed, what truly defined my years with the State Department were the friendships: lasting relationships forged in high-threat environments. They weren't just professional connections; they were lifelines.

And one of them would become something I never saw coming.

CHAPTER 11
CLOSET? WHAT CLOSET?

"The heart has its reasons, which reason knows not." –Blaise Pascal

Erin turned my world upside down. We met in El Salvador, and we bonded over ties to the Midwest, a shared sense of adventure, eerie similarities in our exes, and alcohol.

In 2014, I was grieving the loss of my father, and Erin was there, steady and present when I needed someone to anchor me. She became part of a multi-layered midlife crisis that involved a new tattoo, a motorcycle, a haircut, and a realization that surprised no one—except me. And my mother.

So, at the ripe old age of forty-two, I came out. I would say, "came out of the closet," but I had never been in the closet. I hadn't allowed myself to consider it.

It took me years longer than it should have to admit that my marriage to the drill sergeant wasn't working—that it wasn't a relationship where I could grow, nor one I wanted to bring children into. In the end, I spent twenty years in that unhealthy relationship before finally deciding I deserved better. I had divorced the drill sergeant when I departed Kuwait. Then I remarried him a few years later, only to divorce him again.

During the time between marriages, I did not date anyone. I told myself it was because I was scared of what I would find out there. Maybe it had more to do with the fact that deep down, I knew I would not find what I was looking for in the places I was looking.

I buried myself in work and played the part: tough, strong, decisive, hetero-normative woman.

I got pretty good at keeping people at arm's length. Years in law enforcement and diplomacy had trained me to compartmentalize—stay calm, stay focused, don't let it get too personal.

When I fell for Erin, my armor started to crack. In an effort to spend as much time with her as possible, I suggested we train together to run a marathon. Erin was not a runner, so we settled on a 5k and began jogging together before work. I knew I was crazy about her; I just had no idea whether she was crazy about me, or I was just going crazy. Eventually it became clear the feeling was mutual.

Erin came into my life like a wrecking ball, impossible to ignore. She didn't push, but she never backed down. I had spent decades building my walls, but before I knew what was happening, they had crumbled.

To my surprise, I liked it. I felt—safe.

Erin was with me on that epic night lost in Honduras. Somehow, we came out the other side of the storm and the darkness, and neither of us had lost our cool. That's when I knew we could survive anything, together.

We got married in Hawaii in 2017. No big production, just the two of us on a beach with her sister and brother-in-law. It was quiet and grounding, like something solid had finally clicked into place. A piece of myself that I hadn't even been aware of had been waiting for me to recognize and claim it.

45

CHAPTER 12

THE COST OF ARMOR

"In a time of deceit, telling the truth is a revolutionary act." –
George Orwell

Over the next few years, I settled into the quiet understanding that being gay was simply one part of who I was—neither the entire story, nor a defect to correct.

I reflected on how identity can shape what we're willing to question, about ourselves and about our world. Were there other parts of me I had not been true to?

I'd been a tomboy as long as I could recall. I hated dresses, didn't play with dolls, and preferred trips to Radio Shack with Dad over clothes shopping with Mom. I wanted to be tough, not cute and fragile. As a kid, I remember wanting to be a boy—not because I disliked who I was, but because that was the lane where I could be strong, adventurous, and free. It was where there were no dresses or dolls.

I carried that tough identity into college and beyond. I prided myself on being resilient. In the worlds I came to occupy, it served me well. Early in my career, toughness was a prerequisite and a badge of honor.

In the police academy, I figured the quickest way to earn respect was to be one of the guys and to prove I didn't need special accommodations. When it came time for the fitness test, I refused to do the "hang" offered to female recruits. I grabbed the bar and knocked out twenty pull-ups.

As a newly credentialed DS agent, in 2004, I volunteered to do a six-week assignment on President Hamid Karzai's protection detail in Afghanistan. Before I left, my supervisor pulled me aside and informed me, "The Afghan government asked us not to send any female agents."

She made it clear that the choice was mine. I didn't hesitate; I was going.

I had no issues gaining the respect of my male Afghan colleagues then, nor fourteen years later when I returned as a Division Chief of Investigations and Vetting, supervising nearly fifty Afghan men.

During that first assignment, I accompanied President Karzai on a visit to Bamiyan Province. Before his arrival, we were greeted by Governor Habiba Sarobi—the first and only female governor in Afghanistan. She stood on the steps of the government building, firmly instructing the men to maintain order during the visit. The crowd listened. In a country where most women were still wrapped head to toe, here was one commanding authority without apology.

When I returned in 2018, several strong young Afghan women worked for me as FSNIs alongside their male counterparts. Fierce, intelligent, and ambitious, they reminded me of that moment on the steps in Bamiyan—of what could be possible if only they were given the chance.

When the country fell in 2021, they all had to flee. They were brilliant, capable, and determined, yet survival meant disappearing.

Throughout my career, I was often the only woman: in campus security at CofO, as a volunteer firefighter, on my squad at SAPD, on protection details and in war zones with DSS. Even when I wasn't the only one, we were always the minority.

I was in my forties before I reached the point where I was comfortable enough with my accomplishments that I no longer felt I had to prove myself in every new environment or situation. My reputation could stand on its own. It was liberating.

At fifty, I began to sense that there were gentler, more nurturing parts of me that had slipped through the cracks over time, buried beneath armor I thought I needed to wear. I finally began to realize that the strength I had relied on for so long didn't need to be so hard-edged.

I wondered if other women felt the same. Some of the strongest, sharpest, most capable people I had ever served with were women. Yet I couldn't recall having this conversation with any of them. Were they all carrying this kind of unspoken weight?

Maybe the draw to be one of the guys isn't the same for the generation of women behind me. Maybe they've found more room for balance. I hope so.

And yet, I don't know if I would change a thing. All those years being one of the guys—I loved it. I never would have survived without them.

Some of my closest friends remain the men I served alongside. I still carry their respect with me, and I carry it with reverence. Those friendships—many of them forged in pressure, in danger, in deep camaraderie—remain sacred to me. I was supported, included, and respected. I had found my place among men who didn't ask me to be anything but competent and loyal. They didn't just have my six; they valued me for myself, even before I fully knew who that was.

Nevertheless, there was a cost to all those years of being tough. The very traits that earned me respect—composure, grit, and detachment—were the same ones that kept me from noticing the toll stress was taking on my body.

The shortness of breath, the increasing jaw pain, the chronic cough that came and went, and finally the numbing with alcohol, were all manifestations of stress. I ignored the root cause, letting my armor separate me from my own body.

I once heard that the reason first responders and military members are eligible for retirement after only twenty years is that few of us would make it much longer. The job takes years from us, and heart attacks, cancers, autoimmune disease, and suicide claim too many too soon.

We swallow what we aren't allowed to say, and we call it strength. But the stress keeps settling in, layer by layer.

CHAPTER 13

SANCTUARY

"Someone's sitting in the shade today because someone planted a tree a long time ago." –Warren Buffett

---

Like most people, when COVID arrived and the world fell apart in 2020, I was initially terrified. After my extreme bout with bronchitis in the police academy, I got a round of it every year. I had struggled with a chronic cough both the entire year I was in Iraq and the year I was in Afghanistan. I assumed it was the pollution. More than once, my lung infections had come close to putting me in the hospital.

When the State Department authorized employees to leave overseas postings and ride out the pandemic elsewhere, Erin and I didn't hesitate. The construction site in Hermosillo, Mexico, where I was working as Site Security Manager, had shut down. Erin's job had also moved to remote work. There was nothing keeping us there.

So we packed up the dogs, loaded the car with supplies (including toilet paper) and drove twenty-four hours straight from Mexico to the Ozarks.

The apocalypse movies have it all wrong. When it hits the fan, the highways aren't clogged with abandoned cars; they are empty. For miles, it was only us, the open road, and the occasional semi-truck. Not a single patrol car in sight. Gas stations were deserted—just flickering neon signs buzzing in the stillness.

We stopped only for gas and didn't use indoor restrooms. One benefit of no cars on the road? There's no one to see you squatting on the shoulder. After all, there was plenty of toilet paper in the car.

We spent around six months at The Middle Ground. As the world descended into COVID-era madness, we watched from the tranquility of the Ozarks.

Parks were closed. Grocery stores had arrows taped to the floors like some dystopian board game. Lone paddle-boarders and fishermen were arrested or fined. Outdoor mask mandates were issued. Plexiglas barriers floated uselessly in midair. Restaurant staff enforced mask mandates between the door and the table, but diners could remove their masks the moment they sat down. Meanwhile, we had sunshine, fresh air, and freedom.

Aside from the quiet escape from all the noise of the world, our time away gave us another unexpected gift. One day, I was out running errands with my brother Rees, who had been taking care of The Middle Ground while I was overseas. He stopped on the side of the road to say hello to a guy he knew who was out mowing. (Yes, this really still happens in the Ozarks.)

As we were pulling out, the man casually added, "Oh, by the way, I'm thinking of selling the property. If you know anyone who might be interested, let me know."

We hadn't gotten a mile down the road before I turned to Rees, grinning. "I have an idea!"

The property for sale had a small hunting cabin that sat on thirty-six acres of land dotted with towering pine trees. To say the cabin was "rustic" was putting it kindly. However, we saw potential for it to be a "rustic chic" getaway for people who wanted a break from places that might feel too oppressive—a chance for others to experience what we had enjoyed during the lock-downs, when even outdoor activities were off-limits in some places.

Erin and I bought the land and dove headfirst into transforming the tiny cabin into a sanctuary. Every detail mattered. We hung artwork that had been given to us over the years by friends, each one carrying a memory or a story. Somehow, the pieces fit together effortlessly, like they had always been meant to come together in that place.

The final touch was the mantel from my childhood home—a perfect bridge between past and present.

CHAPTER 14
PANDEMICS AND PARADIGM SHIFTS

"Condemnation without investigation is the height of ignorance." –Albert Einstein

We returned to Mexico as Operation Warp Speed was in full swing and vaccine trials sped up at a breakneck pace. The world was shifting quickly and dramatically, which I had experienced before, but something about it seemed different this time. I began to question and reevaluate at a level I never had before.

From the start, something about the COVID pandemic didn't sit right with me, though not in a way I could articulate at the time. When talk of a vaccine began, the thought of taking it triggered a visceral, full-body panic. I couldn't explain that somatic-level response, but I also couldn't reason it away.

In my work, gut instinct mattered. When something didn't add up, I paid attention. I'd spent years assessing risk and making decisions under pressure, and this was no different. For reasons I didn't yet understand, my body was telling me to pause.

I wasn't "anti-vax." Due to my work, I'd taken vaccines many people never get, like rabies and even anthrax; but it was always after weighing the risks for myself. The only one I'd routinely declined was the flu shot, after a severe reaction in 2003 left me nearly hospitalized. I'd never had a serious case of the flu since, and with COVID initially resembling a severe flu, I couldn't justify the risk.

Early in the pandemic, my doctor asked if there was any family history of vaccine reactions. I reached out to both biological parents. My birth mother shared that she'd had a severe reaction to a flu vaccine while pregnant with me—so severe she developed a chronic condition, and her declining health was part of her decision not to keep me. That revelation certainly didn't ease my concern.

My doctor agreed that with my family and personal history, I had a legitimate medical reason to decline. She agreed to support an exemption if needed. But when the time came, she hesitated. "Perhaps a religious exemption would be the way to go?"

At first I was angry that I was being forced to justify what my body already knew, through a method that felt insincere. But eventually, I realized that I did hold a sincere belief, rooted in something far older than any religious institution. At my core, I believed humanity's arrogance in trying to improve upon nature would come at a cost. I believed in natural immunity. I believed in my body's ability to fight off disease. I believed in my absolute right to choose what went into my body.

I also felt betrayed by an employer I had served for nearly two decades. I had spent over nine years overseas in Iraq, Uganda, El Salvador, Afghanistan, and Mexico, risking life and limb in the service of my country. Now, all of that meant nothing if I didn't comply? It was an impossible choice.

I spent hours each day immersed in scientific papers and congressional hearings, trying to understand what was happening, where I stood, and what to do about it.

I joined the Federal Law Enforcement Officers' Association (FLEOA) and consulted legal counsel, hoping to delay termination long enough to reach retirement eligibility in January 2024.

With no formal religious affiliation, I joined an online church I heard about on "The Survival Podcast," a show I followed for permaculture and homesteading topics. One of the church's declarations read: "I believe all humans have sovereign rights to their body, what is done to their body and what goes or does not go into it. This right is absolute."

I submitted my religious exemption, updated my resume, and prepared for the worst. I was prepared to walk away from it all, if it really came to that.

Facing the possibility of no more keeping one ear open for radio traffic, no more crisis calls in the middle of the night, and no more assignments, questions tumbled through my mind: *Who am I without my credentials? Can I really walk away?*

I turned my focus to the only thing I could still do: push back. Alongside other Department of State employees, I co-wrote a Dissent Channel cable, an internal tool for raising serious policy concerns.

I also joined a lawsuit against the federal government with a newly formed group called Feds for Medical Freedom (F4MF). The conflict weighed on me in ways I hadn't expected. It wasn't only fear of losing my career. It was the realization that I could not live in a world where my bodily autonomy felt negotiable.

Years of service and dedication suddenly felt disposable, reduced to a single personal decision I believed was mine alone to make. In one dark, unmoored moment, when fear gained far too much control of my thinking thanks to the influence of alcohol, I considered an escape that would mean never having to choose at all.

The fact that I had been pushed to that point shook me—and it made me furious. Anger replaced despair. I decided I would not break. I would not trade autonomy for comfort, nor integrity for compliance.

In a moment of desperation, I convinced myself that getting COVID would help me qualify for a natural-immunity argument in court. I visited a friend who was miserably sick, sat across from him at his kitchen table for over an hour while he coughed and wheezed, then went home and waited. Imagine being disappointed not to get COVID.

My plan failed, and Erin was justifiably furious that I had tried to catch a contagious disease without consulting her.

Looking back, it wasn't just the mandates that felt suffocating. It was the heaviness in the air, as though the world had gone into a trance. The level of quiet compliance made me question not only the rules, but my own place within them. For me, refusing wasn't about politics; it was simply preserving my health and autonomy. I knew what was right for me, and I respected that others made different choices.

The possibility of losing my hard-won career as a Supervisory Special Agent and diplomat began to seep into everything—my body, my home, my marriage. At that point, I decided to reach out to my inner circle and do something I thought I'd never have to do again: come out.

In 2014, when I had finally accepted that I had no choice but to go public with my relationship with Erin, I was terrified. I worried that friends and colleagues would shun me. I didn't give people enough credit, or maybe I'm exceptionally skilled at choosing high-quality friends. Either way, only two high-school friends and my mother expressed discomfort with my announcement. Meanwhile, most of my friends had figured it out long before I did.

Coming out as "unvaxxed" was harder than I expected. Being gay had taught me that people often assume your politics, but I had never fit into any box. My views were shaped by what I had seen, experienced, and learned. As the pandemic dragged on, I heard people I respected make casual, cutting remarks about the unvaccinated—comments that landed like gut punches. The fact that the issue fell along political lines at all baffled me.

I kept wondering: would they be as rigid in their views if they knew Erin and I had also had reservations because she was taking fertility drugs? That we were trying to get pregnant? That we had already endured one failed attempt and one miscarriage? How could we introduce something new into her body and never know if it had played a role in another loss?

Anxiety became my constant companion. The inability to take a full breath returned. Sleep slipped away. I had never felt so ostracized and othered. I was angry, at everything. I was drinking daily, not to unwind, but to numb.

So I began telling friends that I would not take the vaccine. Some quietly supported my choice, often confiding that they also had felt coerced. One admitted that it felt like selling his soul to cave to the pressure. Only one supported the mandate, and we agreed to disagree.

To be reminded that I had such loyal, non-judgmental friends was a reprieve from the pressure and a lifeline in a world that felt hostile.

Then, on January 21, 2022, a ruling came down in the F4MF case: U.S. District Court Judge Jeffrey Vincent Brown of the Southern District of Texas issued a nationwide injunction against the federal employee mandate.

It didn't undo the damage, but for the first time in months, I could breathe.

CHAPTER 15
CHINGONA

I've said before that the military probably wouldn't have been a good fit for me. Not because I wanted to be difficult, but because I've always had the reflex to ask, "Is this necessary? Is it just?"

As I moved up through the ranks in DSS, that instinct only sharpened. By the time I was a Supervisory Special Agent, I'd learned that real leadership sometimes meant pushing back—especially when a policy hurt the people I was responsible for.

That was certainly the case with the mask mandates. They became a symbol of misplaced priorities, prioritizing optics over common sense and staff well-being. When the CDC dropped its recommendation for outdoor masking and the Department followed suit, I told my staff they could ditch the masks on patrol, where they walked the fence line of a six-acre compound—alone.

So I was surprised when my supervisor, the acting project director, wanted to keep the outdoor requirement in place. I asked what authority he had to do that. When it became clear the answer was "none," I refused to impose requirements that had no basis in current health guidance or law. I reminded him that my team was walking the perimeter for hours in triple-digit heat, sometimes six days a week.

From then on, the team wore masks only when the acting project director was on site. They'd watch for his vehicle and key their radios to pass along the unspoken warning: mask up. A quiet rebellion.

Months later, when the CDC and the Department loosened the rules for masking indoors, he still refused to adopt the change. I kept my distance, working behind a closed door whenever possible. Then one day in a meeting, he told me to put a mask on.

It escalated.

I stood my ground, then finally excused myself from the meeting. That is the only time in my career that I recall losing my composure at work. Later that day, he told me he thought I was a poor leader for not enforcing his policies.

When my tour in Hermosillo ended, my team threw me a farewell party at a local watering hole. It was an evening of hugs, laughter, and camaraderie, with not a single mask in sight. It was one of the best send-offs of my career.

They gave me a hard hat covered in messages. One stood out: "Kemmi, La LGF reconoce tu calidad, como persona, como líder... sabemos que donde estés... serás CHINGONA!!" Which translates to: "Kemmi, The LGF recognizes your strength—as a person, as a leader. Wherever you go, you will be the CHINGONA!!"

I raised an eyebrow. "Chingona?"

They grinned. "One bad-ass woman."

I left Hermosillo with my head high, reminded that leadership isn't about blind obedience. It's about doing the right thing for your people.

CHAPTER 16
THE VINE OF SOULS

"When the student is ready, the teacher appears." –Buddhist Proverb

With concerns over continuing to be treated as an "other" in many places around the globe, including areas of the United States, I bid on an onward assignment as the Resident Agent in Charge of the Orlando Pilot Office.

It was both a strategic move to a place with minimal restrictions, and the perfect final assignment, bookending my law enforcement career by returning to Florida where it had all started.

Surrounded by fresh air and sunshine, I relaxed for the first time in nearly two years. The crushing anxiety in my chest dissipated. I stopped drinking every night, dropping to a mere four or five nights a week. My diet choices improved slightly.

I set a goal to lose my "COVID 19," the weight I had put on by drinking and stress eating the previous two years. I entertained thoughts of walking the Camino de Santiago in Spain when I retired, and began walking an hour or more every morning in preparation.

And, perhaps most importantly, I consumed less COVID-related news. For the first time in years, I listened for enjoyment. That's when I stumbled across The Joe Rogan Experience.

And that's when my journey from the badge to the vine got started.

Joe Rogan and Graham Hancock were talking about an ancient Amazonian brew—"eye-a-waska"—a conduit to ancient wisdom. Graham said it let you speak with the ancestors, confront your ego, and receive spiritual instruction from something far wiser than yourself.

I hit pause, rewound, and wrote the word phonetically on a notepad like it was a clue in an investigation. Once I got the spelling right, the search results exploded.

I devoured articles, books, documentaries, and first-person accounts from veterans, researchers, and skeptics. I read Terence McKenna, Michael Pollan, Rick Doblin, Jeremy Narby, and others. I wanted to know what it was, how it worked, and why it worked.

And—if I'm honest—why I suddenly couldn't stop thinking about it.

I'd never touched a drug in my life, not even weed. As a young police officer, I had confiscated pot from teenagers and told them to get their lives together. Only in recent years had I accepted that marijuana might have medical value.

But this was different. The moment I heard the word *ayahuasca*, a deep yearning lit up inside me.

One day at a friend's house I noticed a framed cross-stitch that had hung on her wall for years, but never caught my eye. It displayed Genesis 1:29: "Behold, I have given you every plant yielding seed... You shall have them for food."

Every plant? Including the ones that change your consciousness? If God made them, didn't that mean they were here for a reason?

I'd been on the other side of the story—The War on Drugs, "Just Say No." I started to wonder: who benefits from keeping these plants illegal? And more importantly—who loses? Shouldn't access to nature be between a person and their Creator?

Of all the psychedelics I researched, ayahuasca stood out. It was sacred, demanding, and intelligent. It wasn't for escape—it was for healing. Not a "trip," but a reckoning.

Indigenous cultures in the Amazon had been brewing it for centuries. Some call her Mother Ayahuasca. Some, a guide. Others, a surgeon with roots for hands who slices through your ego like butter. She shows you what you need to see, and she's not subtle. She can be terrifying or show you beauty. Sometimes both.

The more I learned, the more I understood that this was not something to be taken lightly. It demanded respect—for the sacrament, the process, and the lineage. It would require me to relinquish control and face myself honestly, yet somehow I was not deterred.

My subconscious craved that very thing after years of maintaining control and not looking too closely.

I found a center in Orlando offering ceremonies for first responders, and joined the waitlist while exploring backup options in South America. I told myself that if ayahuasca was truly calling, the invitation would come.

Meanwhile, I was enjoying life in Florida, reconnecting with old friends, meeting new friends, and thoroughly enjoying my job again— so much so that I considered extending for another year. After all, it wasn't my DSS leadership who had tried to fire me. In fact, no one from DSS had ever mentioned mandates to me. Yet, despite my awareness that the pressure to push me out had come from higher up the chain, trust and mutual respect had been lost.

I also knew that amidst the turmoil, something within me was ready for change. I was ready to start a new chapter—one where I no longer had to fight battles I didn't want to fight. The time had come to reclaim my peace and maybe even return to myself and to the people who loved me. I knew at some level that the stress from work, the emotional overload, and the unresolved grief I carried were all leaking out of me at home.

———

One of the obvious perks of living in Orlando was its proximity to Disney. It is Erin's favorite place to spend money—sorry, time.

She got a season pass and went at every opportunity, which was often. Her best friend from college lived in Fort Lauderdale and often drove up with her kids. They spent weekends at the parks, going on the same rides, doing the same things again and again. I saw it as Erin returning to a place and time in her life when things were uncomplicated, reclaiming something she'd once lost.

Occasionally I'd tag along, if the crowds were projected to be light. One weekend, another couple came with the family. As they explored the park, ayahuasca came up in conversation. The husband casually mentioned he had taken part in an ayahuasca ceremony somewhere deep in the woods of south Florida. Over dinner, I listened intently as Brad, a firefighter, detailed his experience.

For him, most of it had been a flood of memories: tragic scenes from years of calls as a first-responder. He heard sirens and processed moments of chaos and loss.

It had been quite a few years since his ceremony, and he did not care to return, but he also did not regret it. That intensely emotional experience was ultimately a positive one where he had found healing.

He also mentioned that he could put me in touch with his contact.

I nearly dropped my $22 margarita. After all my searching, all my research, all my waiting—this landed in my lap. And at the "most magical place on Earth," no less.

CHAPTER 17
BREAKING THE SILENCE

"You are not required to set yourself on fire to keep others warm." –Unknown

In 2023, a few months before retiring, I finally got the chance to attend the Women in Federal Law Enforcement (WIFLE) conference in Tampa. I'd thrown my name in the hat many times before, hoping to make it at least once before leaving law enforcement.

Moving from session to session, I saw something I'd never witnessed in my career—open, honest conversations about trauma. Not only firsthand trauma, the kind you experience on a scene, but vicarious trauma that seeps in when you're helping others, especially children.

To hear it acknowledged, addressed, and taken seriously gave me genuine hope for the future of the profession I loved and was preparing to leave.

I attended the awards ceremony in support of my colleague, DSS Special Agent Ashley Day, who was receiving the Julie Y. Cross Award for exceptional courage and heroism. Ashley served at the U.S. Embassy in Colombo, Sri Lanka, during the 2022 economic crisis. As violent protests erupted, she coordinated emergency operations that evacuated over two hundred people, including fifty children, from the Overseas School of Colombo. Despite extreme staff shortages, she stayed behind, escorting others to safety, sometimes using evasive driving maneuvers to escape armed mobs.

The second recipient of the award, Special Agent Rhiannon Mancinelli of NCIS, had survived a hostage situation in Humble, Texas. During a domestic violence case, a suspect stormed into his home with a gun and used his daughter as a human shield while firing at Mancinelli and her partner. Mancinelli returned fire and wounded the suspect without harming the child. She then carried both her partner, who had been shot multiple times, and the child to safety.

When Rhiannon took the podium, she didn't talk about tactics. She said, "We need to accept we are not okay. And that it's okay to not be okay."

The room rose in a standing ovation. Everyone there knew what she meant without the need for her to expand: decisions we make on the job leave wounds that do not easily heal.

I thought back to my own early days in law enforcement. At SAPD, five days out of training, I was in an officer-involved shooting. A fender bender turned into a take-down of three murder suspects from California. One was shot.

I didn't fire my weapon that day. Another officer shot the suspect before I could get a round off. Or had I hesitated?

The armed suspect had run into a dimly lit hallway. The gun was small, no larger than the palm of his hand. I yelled, "drop the gun!" So I knew he had one, but I didn't shoot. I remember thinking later, *What an odd feeling to regret not shooting someone.*

That night, I was required to speak with a counselor for a few minutes. That was it.

The next day when I showed up for work, an experienced officer said, "I'm impressed. I didn't think you'd be back."

It was a compliment. I felt proud. He was as hard as nails, and his words conveyed a message: the way to earn respect is through being tough. If you can't handle it, this is not the line of work for you.

For months, the scene replayed like an old film reel—grainy, unrelenting, looping over and over every time I closed my eyes.

I learned from the Florida Department of Law Enforcement (FDLE) that the suspect had pulled the trigger. A round was in the chamber. The firing pin had been struck, leaving a clear indentation on the back of the round.

The only reason I was still standing was because the bullet had been a dud.

I began to have nightmares. One night, I woke up screaming, tears streaming down my face. My skull was open, exposing my brain matter. A surgeon hovered over me, using tweezers to remove tiny pellets of buckshot. Every time he pulled one out, I screamed in pain.

I didn't tell anyone about the nightmare. You didn't talk about such things. I put my uniform on and I kept going to work. I "moved on."

Some time later, I was given a Certificate of Commendation for exceptional courage in the line of duty. I didn't believe I deserved it. I felt like a coward.

The drill sergeant suggested I hang it in the bathroom. I had tried to talk with him after the event, trying to process my actions and feelings. He had said, "If you act tough, be tough." End of conversation.

Nearly twenty-four years had passed since then. Hearing Rhiannon's story—and seeing the response to her words—was a turning point. It forced me to look at my career, my wounds, and the unspoken burden so many first responders carry.

I thought about the steps DSS had taken over the years to address stress and the challenges of the job—most notably, creating a Peer Support Group. It was a network of fellow agents willing to pick up the phone, listen, and walk beside you through the hard times. That effort had always been fully supported by DS leadership during my career. I suspected we were in the minority among federal agencies.

Listening to the conversations at WIFLE, I felt a shift in the mindset industry-wide—one that gave me hope that what had long been the exception might soon become the norm.

As a police recruit, I had memorized *The Law Enforcement Officers Code of Ethics*. We stood as a class and recited it every morning, along with The Pledge of Allegiance. The first line reads: "As a law enforcement officer my fundamental duty is to serve mankind."

I didn't have to carry a badge and a gun to be of service. What if I built a space where groups could come to find sanctuary, heal, grow, and connect with nature?

I already knew that our mountain was special. At our little cabin, guests often left notes about the healing they felt sitting on the porch, watching the valley stretch out before them. Now I began to wonder whether that land might one day help others in my profession find what they'd buried or lost along the way.

I wanted to give others what I wished I'd had all those years ago when I woke up screaming in the middle of the night: a space where it was okay to not be okay.

CHAPTER 18
CELDV

"The mind that opens to a new idea never returns to its original size." –Albert Einstein

---

After receiving the information for Brad's contact, I immediately reached out. In response, I got an invitation to apply to join a church called Centro Espiritualista Luz Do Vegetal (CELDV).

Wait, what?

I just wanted to drink ayahuasca, reach enlightenment, maybe heal from some old wounds—not sign up for Sunday services. I was not looking for organized religion. I had spent my life resisting institutions who claimed to hold the answers.

I submitted the application anyway.

There were many questions about my health, particularly questions about my mental health and any use of psychiatric medications (answer: none, past or present). I was surprised by the thoroughness of the questionnaire.

Having seemingly passed the medical and mental health screening, I received another email. This one asked if I would commit to following the church's guidelines in the days and weeks leading up to taking the sacrament.

Sacrament?

This was all starting to feel more religious than I expected, way beyond just joining an online church to check a box. Brad hadn't mentioned a church, a temple, or a sacrament.

I read through the guidelines describing *la Dieta*, a special diet said to prepare the body for the experience. I was determined to keep an open mind, but it felt like another set of rules. No alcohol, no caffeine, no sugar, no processed food, no red meat or pork. And no sex. A purification of the mind, body, and spirit, they called it.

A few days later, I received a schedule of upcoming ceremonies. Before booking and fully committing to this church, I did what I do best: investigate.

The first email had explained that CELDV followed the teachings of Mestre Gabriel and conducted ceremonies in a temple in south Florida. They were a closed community, growing only through referrals from existing members. In this way, they ensured that the church grew organically from within.

My search led me to José Gabriel da Costa, the founder of Uniao Do Vegetal (UDV)—a Brazilian spiritual movement that began in 1961, blending Christian teachings with the ritual use of ayahuasca. Mestre Gabriel wasn't a priest or a dogmatist. He was a seeker—someone who had ventured into the jungle, found something profound, and felt compelled to share it.

From these roots, the Centro Espiritualista Luz Do Vegetal (CELDV) Church was founded on June 29, 1996, by Mestre Asplinger Alves Feitozas. It was a non-profit Christian religious organization that practiced and spread Mestre Gabriel's message through the sacramental use of ayahuasca, a sacred blend of Amazonian plants believed to expand consciousness and promote spiritual evolution. With the motto "Light, Peace, and Love," CELDV operated its main temple in Manaus, Brazil, and distributed the sacrament in select Brazilian cities and in the United States.

In 2015, Mestre Asplinger traveled to Florida to conduct an ayahuasca ceremony. Shortly after, he recommended to the board of directors in Brazil that a permanent branch be established there. On January 1, 2016, CELDV was officially registered as a non-profit in Florida.

All right, so seemingly not a cult.

Next, I researched *la Dieta*. I had assumed it was about self-discipline —a test of commitment before drinking ayahuasca. As I read more, I understood there were scientific and spiritual reasons behind it.

Meat and processed foods take too much energy to digest, energy that could be used for healing. Caffeine, sugar, and stimulants keep the nervous system in overdrive, making it more difficult to connect with the Divine. Alcohol and other substances create blockages, both energetically and emotionally, making it harder to reach deeper levels of clarity. Even sex and over-stimulation are avoided because they drain the life force energy needed for deeper introspection.

It made sense. Without caffeine, my thoughts would slow down. Without alcohol, I would be forced to sit with my emotions instead of numbing them. Without sugar, I would stop reaching for quick hits of pleasure. Without the noise of daily distractions, I'd have no choice but to listen to the "still, small voice" within.

Beyond the science, there was also symbolism. *La Dieta* wasn't about denial—it was about devotion and reverence.

I pulled up the schedule of ceremonies again. They offered three-day retreats and one-day retreats each month. I wasn't sure I was ready for a full weekend, so I started small and booked my spot for one night.

No meat, no booze, no sugar, no sex, for thirty days. Easy, right?

CHAPTER 19
THE SPACE BETWEEN

"But I have promises to keep, and miles to go before I sleep." –
Robert Frost

Retirement wasn't a single moment. It wasn't the clean break I'd imagined: setting down my gun and badge, walking away without looking back.

Instead, it was an unraveling. A slow, deliberate unwinding of everything that had defined me for over two decades. A shedding of skin, layer by layer, until I wasn't sure what remained underneath.

The Department issued me retirement credentials, but only after I mailed in my active ones. For the first time in twenty-six years, I was without a badge.

The day I sealed that FedEx envelope, my hands trembled. My chest tightened. The moment the package left my grip, something cracked open inside me: a slow, rising panic, and a wave of grief I hadn't expected.

I had spent a lifetime carrying the badge, and now, for the first time, I wasn't sure how to *be* without it.

I'd wager every cop out there knows the game, "Where are my creds?" Erin and I played it often, to her dismay. I'd reach my hand around to my back pocket and panic when I didn't feel the leather wallet that carried my special agent credentials, driver's license, credit card, insurance card, lucky silver dollar, and a $100 bill in case of emergency. We'd search the car, the house, my bag, until we found them and order was restored to my universe.

I'd carried credentials everywhere I went since 1998. I mean everywhere. I was never without my "creds" and rarely without a gun on my hip.

The week it took to get my retirement credentials was excruciating—especially since I made a cross-country drive from Florida to the Ozarks that week. What if I got pulled over and had no badge to show?

I didn't want to be seen as another person in the crowd—a "normal citizen." The thought of flying without a badge, without a gun, without the quiet authority that had shaped my presence for decades, unsettled me. For twenty years, I had flown armed. Now, I would stand in the TSA line the same as everyone else. No bypassing security. No nods of deference.

On one rare occasion when I had traveled without my gun, I had been randomly selected for enhanced screening. I was already on a short fuse, fueled by the COVID restrictions and the intense feelings of oppression I felt during that time.

I became visibly upset at being singled out. I pointed out that normally I didn't go through screening at all, so subjecting me to additional screening made no sense. Something about it felt deeply personal, as if my integrity were being questioned. When it was over and I'd made a complete asshat of myself, I went to the airport bar and pounded two twenty-ounce beers. I was halfway through the second one before the shaking stopped and my heart rate returned to normal levels.

I'm not proud of how I handled that interaction, and I'm grateful the TSA officials that day took my outburst in stride. In hindsight, it reveals how tightly wound I'd become, and how much of my identity was tied not only to the badge, but also to the respect and status the badge commanded.

In retirement, unstructured time became both a luxury and a challenge. I was grateful to have my new business and be able to shift my focus to building both the physical and the intangible foundations of my vision: a space where first responders could come to decompress and heal.

PART THREE
BREAKING THE HUSK

CHAPTER 20
AMEL

"There is no greater love than to lay down one's life for one's friends." –John 15:13, New Living Translation

Amel haunted the quiet corners of my heart. She hadn't been just a colleague. She had been a gentle, generous soul—sharp-minded, soft-spoken, and fiercely loyal in a place where loyalty could get you killed.

I supervised Amel in Baghdad. She was one of our FSNIs, part of a team of local Iraqis who risked their lives daily to support the embassy. If the wrong people found out where they worked, it was a death sentence, and they came to work anyway. They were brave in ways most people will never have to be.

Amel and her husband, Hazim, had the means and the opportunity to leave Iraq. Instead, they stayed, because they believed they still had something to give.

Amel spoke fondly of Iraq before Saddam, of a time when people went about their daily lives without fear, dressed sharply, sought out higher education, and were modern and progressive. She held hope for a return to those days. She wanted that future for her country and wanted to work towards it.

One day Amel and Hazim decided to walk to a bank several neighborhoods away to collect several months' worth of pension payments on behalf of a friend living outside of Iraq. It should have been a routine errand.

The bank was closed due to military activity in the area, but the guard let them in. The manager processed the withdrawal. As they stepped onto the street, young men dressed in black approached and demanded the money. Then they told Amel and Hazim they had to pay a fine for being Christian, and they took Hazim.

Amel clung to him, tried to pull him back. But there was nothing she could do. They drove off, leaving her screaming for help.

They called her minutes later from Hazim's phone and told her to return to the bank. When she did, they took her purse, tossed Hazim's phone at her feet, and disappeared.

Inside her purse, in a side pocket, were her U.S. Embassy ID and International Zone badge. In Iraq, those weren't credentials. They were a death sentence.

What had likely begun as a shakedown had now turned into something far more dangerous.

I connected her with a team working on hostage cases to assist her with the negotiations. We tried to buy time, exploring every option we could think of. She carried three phones everywhere she went. I sat with Amel and another Iraqi co-worker as Amel scrolled through the ringtones searching for one that would get her attention no matter what. I don't recall exactly what was behind her choice, but maybe in the moment, it made things a little less scary. So the phone that rang with a baby's laugh was for "them"—the kidnappers—and whenever we heard it, we all froze.

The kidnappers first demanded $250,000. Negotiations went on for some time, and I secured lodging for her on the embassy compound. I took her to the medical unit and tried to make sure she was eating and sleeping.

One day, they finally let Hazim speak to her. He told her, "Amel, please pay them. Pay them $30,000."

The deal was sealed. They knew she could raise that amount. In fact, she had already collected that much from friends and colleagues.

She didn't want to wait any longer, believing that if she didn't go, they would kill Hazim.

She told me, "Kemmi, this is my destiny. I am ready."

I hugged her at the gates of the embassy, hoping it wouldn't be the last time I saw her.

I'm not at liberty to share the details of what happened next. But I can say that whatever systems she believed would protect her—failed.

Several excruciating weeks passed. Then word came that two unidentified bodies had been discovered in a Baghdad morgue. Amel's U.S. Embassy badge had been found on her body, with her name on the front and mine on the back, listed as her American supervisor. That was the detail that alerted local authorities to contact the Embassy. It was also the detail that broke something inside me: the illusion that I could protect anyone.

Ambassador Ryan Crocker later told the embassy community, "Security forces tried to track her. Lost her. And two of their own."

It wasn't supposed to happen this way.

I kept asking myself: what could I have done differently? Should I have pleaded harder for her not to go? But how do you stop someone who's fighting to save the love of their life?

I traveled to London to escort their remains and meet their son. The funeral was delayed, but I stayed long enough to sit with him and hear stories of their life together.

Their son looked like both of them. He carried Amel's grace and Hazim's quiet strength. He asked me questions, and I answered what I could. At one point, he said, "Maybe she knew she wouldn't return. Maybe she chose to go with him."

I recalled her words as she walked toward danger: "This is my destiny. I am ready."

Before I returned to Iraq, I visited the funeral home. I sat beside her casket and whispered: "I'm sorry. I hope you can forgive me. I did everything I could. I wish it had been enough."

Organizing Amel's memorial service in Baghdad was one of the hardest things I'd ever done, but we honored her and Hazim the best we could. After Ambassador Crocker spoke, I read "The Road Not Taken," by Robert Frost—a poem that spoke to me of paths, courage, and choosing to walk a road few would dare. Amel had chosen the harder path again and again, not because she had to, but because she believed in something greater. I also spoke of how Amel's name means "hope" in Arabic.

The day before the service was to be held, I was in the FSNI office. We were doing our best to focus on anything other than the grief hanging over us.

Out of the blue, two black birds flew to the window and perched on the iron grate. They stared into the room, still and unwavering. We all froze and watched them in silence.

When they flew away, one of the FSNIs turned to me with tears in her eyes and whispered, "Those were the souls of Amel and Hazim coming to say goodbye."

83

CHAPTER 21
A MISSED CONNECTION

When the time finally arrived to prepare for my first ayahuasca ceremony, I followed *la Dieta* as closely as I could. To my surprise, giving up sugar and news was infinitely harder than giving up alcohol.

Before COVID, I had already cut back significantly on drinking—or at least the kind of drinking I'd done in my twenties and thirties, when I didn't know when to stop and usually just drank until I passed out. In more recent years, I'd learned something like moderation. Still, I'd have a pass-out-drunk night now and then and spend two days recovering, vowing, never again. Several months would go by, something stressful would happen, I'd decide I deserved to "blow off some steam," and the cycle would repeat.

Sometimes this happened with a small group of friends, or at home with Erin. Other times, it was more public.

In 2015, while posted in El Salvador, I agreed to attend the Marine Corps Ball with a couple of girlfriends who were excited to give me a makeover. I bought a dress and sat drinking mimosas while they worked, trying to get relaxed enough to go to the ball. (It was the last time I tried to fit myself into that picture. The next Marine Corps Ball I attended, three years later in Austria with Erin, I wore a tuxedo.)

By the time we arrived at the ball, I was already lit, doing my best not to pass out at the table before dinner was even served. My boss, a trusted friend who had served with me in Iraq in 2006, quietly called for his car and had someone drive me home.

In 2019, the week after Erin and I left our one-year assignment in Afghanistan, we ran into someone I knew from Iraq at a rooftop bar in Washington, D.C. He started buying rounds, and we began trading war stories—the kind that draw people together through shared experience.

I drank until I passed out in the bathroom, slumped on the toilet. This rightly led to a gentle but firm request to leave the premises. Erin ordered an Uber, explaining to the two bouncers holding me upright, "She just left Afghanistan." Their demeanors softened as they helped load me into the car.

In a strange twist of fate, the Uber driver—who had to pull over so I could vomit out the side of the vehicle—was from Afghanistan. He spoke English, but when Erin spoke to him in Dari and apologized, he softened as well.

By the time we reached the hotel, Erin realized she wouldn't be able to get me inside by herself. It was two in the morning when she called one of the agents who had worked for me in Afghanistan and happened to be in D.C.

He came to help his former boss's wife get her into the hotel, because that's what you do. It was humiliating, but a common enough story among my peers. Getting each other home was just part of how we looked out for each other, because alcohol was one of our only acceptable coping mechanisms.

On *la Dieta*, abstaining completely from alcohol was hard enough to make me start questioning my relationship with it. I also noticed that without it, the quality of my sleep drastically improved.

As I made the drive south from Orlando, I reviewed what I hoped to gain from the experience. Much of what I'd read about using psychedelics for healing emphasized setting an intention ahead of time.

Only one? I wondered. How could I narrow it down? I had a list of questions, half of them existential, the other half emotional triage. Narrowing them down was like picking a favorite regret.

What is my path? Am I on it? How do I start over when my entire identity has been tied to the badge? How do I release the anger, cynicism, and constant need to analyze and assess every situation?

And then there were the ones that weighed heaviest on my heart.

Would Dad have supported my relationship with Erin? I'd fallen in love with Erin after my father passed away, and I did not know what his views on homosexuality were. I could take an educated guess, though. He was a devout Mormon all his life.

And yet, I had experienced unconditional love from him. He had been my biggest fan and always supported me wholeheartedly. I wanted to believe he would accept this part of me. My mother had intimated that he would not, saying I dishonored his memory by being with Erin. Maybe ayahuasca would allow me to ask him myself.

Then there was Amel. Did she blame me for not being able to save her? I hoped that ayahuasca would allow me to ask her forgiveness, and know her response.

I really did not know what to expect. I only knew that I was so drawn to the experience that I had to see it through.

I arrived in the late afternoon and was instructed to go around the house to the porch to check in. The email confirming my reservation had explained that everyone would be required to stay overnight to ensure no one risked driving under the effects of the sacrament, and I was assigned Cabin Nine by Inti, one of the church leaders.

The cabin was perfect—just big enough for a single bed and a small writing desk.

The property was so densely wooded that even though the cabins were close together, they still felt private. The whole place radiated tranquility.

Concrete statues lined the pathways among the cabins, a mix of Christian figures and Hindu deities. Outside my cabin stood a little cherub holding a harp with wind chimes for its strings. I ran my finger along the strings as I passed.

I took my sleeping bag to the temple and set up my space toward the rear. The temple stood at the heart of the property, a large screened-in gazebo with a soft, white, sandy floor. Along the walls, eighteen mats were arranged in a circle, each with a small black pail beside it.

Having set up my space, I returned to my cabin to await the ringing of a bell that would signal it was time to begin. I was anxious and tried to meditate.

Meditation was new for me, and it was not going well. I could never seem to stop the chatter in my head. There was always a dialogue going on in there, often as if I were writing in a journal: *The temple was large and had space to accommodate twenty people easily.* After a minute or two, I'd give up trying to shut it off and let my thoughts wander wherever they wanted.

When the bell finally rang, I changed into my white T-shirt and white yoga pants and went to the temple.

I felt silly wearing white. Mormons also wear white when they go to the temple. I had worked so hard to shed that skin, and now here I was, dressed like a ghost from my past.

The ceremony began at dusk. A show of hands revealed that about half of the eighteen participants had been there before. We started with a prayer to Mother Ayahuasca, calling upon the ancestors to guide us on our journey.

In the welcome speech, participants were advised to surrender. The importance of having the right mindset—the mindset of a warrior—was stressed. I told myself, *Bring it on! Don't go easy on me. I can take it.*

When it was my turn to kneel before the altar, butterflies swarmed in my stomach. But I had watched the others, so I moved forward without hesitation and accepted the two-ounce Dixie cup from Inti.

A thick, dirt-brown liquid clung to the sides. It smelled of damp earth and old wood. The taste was both familiar and foreign, with an aftertaste that lingered on my tongue like bark.

At the altar was a bowl of fruit. I took a piece of watermelon, hoping to mask the aftertaste. I returned to my mat and placed my empty cup on the rail above my space, ready in case I wanted more. I sat down to wait for something to happen.

Thirty minutes passed.

I sensed that some others were feeling the effects. By this time, night had fallen, and it was dark out. The temple was lit only by candlelight.

A few people were crying. Others were purging into their little black buckets.

I focused on clearing my mind: *I surrender.*

Nothing.

I felt no strange sensations. I had no unusual thoughts. I saw no visions.

An hour in, Inti asked if I needed more sacrament, and I accepted another cup. The taste had not improved.

Still nothing.

Something inside me refused to give up control. The ancestors did not speak to me. The walls I had spent decades constructing were stronger than I thought.

By the end of the night, I had downed five cups of the bitter brew. Still no visions, no insights, no great awakening. Only nausea after the fourth cup, and frustration after the fifth.

I was devastated. Everyone else, it seemed, had cried, purged, laughed, or seen visions. Meanwhile, I had spent the night staring at the candlelight, waiting for something—anything—to happen. I felt unworthy.

I sought out Inti. "Why didn't it work? Why was I not able to connect?"

He asked me, "Do you smoke a lot of marijuana?"

"No," I replied. "I have never smoked marijuana."

"What do you do for work?"

"I was in law enforcement."

"Ah, that makes sense," he whispered, but it landed with the weight of years.

He explained that it was not uncommon for people in law enforcement, military, and intelligence circles to struggle to connect. He speculated that my years of training, compartmentalizing, and suppressing emotions to always remain in control and to maintain my composure had prevented me from letting my guard down enough for the sacrament to work.

I told myself I had surrendered, but was my ego really willing to let me be vulnerable in a group full of strangers?

Everyone was invited to the porch to share a meal and each other's company, to share what they had experienced. I was not feeling very social, so I returned to my cabin and tried to sleep.

Sleep did not come. I felt so dejected and had so many questions. The next morning, I asked Inti if I should try again. With tears welling up, I told him how strongly I had felt called to ayahuasca. He suggested I come for a three-day retreat. He said gently, "Sometimes, the mind is like a coconut—it takes more than one strike to crack it open."

Ha, I thought. *A coconut wrapped in Kevlar!*

I wasn't sure if that reassured me. Either way, it confirmed my walls were thick as hell.

I spotted a certificate of appreciation on the wall from a veterans' group the church worked with.

"Could I join one of those retreats?" I asked. "Maybe my subconscious would allow me to be vulnerable around others with the same mental barricades."

It was possible, he told me, but there were currently no dates set for a veterans' session.

I left with no answers, but I was not ready to give up. As I drove to Orlando, I turned off the radio. No distractions. Just silence.

I wasn't sure if I would try again. So I did the only thing I could think to do: I whispered a small prayer, the first I'd said in a very long time.

"Mother Ayahuasca, if I am to pursue this path, if I am being called to this; please give me a sign."

CHAPTER 22

CRACKING THE COCONUT

"The wound is the place where the Light enters you." –Rumi

The day after I returned home, I picked up a book I'd been reading. I flipped to the next chapter and laughed out loud at the quote at the top of the page:

"For a seed to achieve its greatest expression, it must come completely undone. The shell cracks, its insides come out, and everything changes. To someone who doesn't understand growth, it would look like complete destruction."

The message couldn't have been clearer. I sent Inti a text and said I'd be booking a spot at the next three-day retreat.

Over the next few days, something shifted. I almost felt the medicine traveling through my neural pathways, softening the barricades I'd built around my compartmentalizations.

I began to remember things I hadn't thought of in years.

There was the case of a five-year old girl in El Salvador. She had been sexually abused by her mother's boyfriend in Virginia. Her mother sent her to live with an aunt in El Salvador—maybe to protect her, maybe to protect him. It wasn't clear.

The boyfriend had sent people to the aunt's house searching for the little girl. The aunt, terrified they would harm her to silence her, brought the child to the U.S. Embassy, desperate for help.

We worked with child protective services in Virginia and arranged for the girl to return to the United States and be placed in foster care. A consular officer from the embassy would accompany her on the flight and turn her over to the authorities once they landed on U.S. soil. My job was to assist the consular officer by assuring Salvadoran immigration authorities that the girl was not being trafficked or otherwise mistreated.

The aunt met us in the airport lobby early in the morning on the day of the flight. Their goodbye was gut-wrenching to watch.

As soon as the aunt left, the little girl became inconsolable. No matter what we tried, she wouldn't come willingly through the security checkpoints. Having no other choice, I picked her up and carried her through as my FSNI explained to airport officials what was happening.

She kicked my ribs. Her tiny fists hammered against my back. Her screams pierced the air like a siren. "¡Ayúdame! ¡Ayúdame!" (Help me. Help me.)

The words burned, each one landing like a blow to the chest as bystanders looked on in horror. She shouted words no five-year-old should know, let alone scream in public. Words my colleague and I hadn't learned in our diplomatic language training.

It took all I had not to fall apart right then and there.

She didn't understand what was happening. I wasn't sure I did either. And this experience—being ripped away from the one person she trusted—would likely be one more trauma on top of what was already too many.

We ended up spending most of the day at the airport, trying to gain her trust. Eventually we coaxed her onto a flight after the first pilot refused to board her—understandably worried that passengers would think she was being kidnapped.

I hadn't thought of that little girl for years.

I had locked that memory away and filed it under, "just doing my job." Now, it sat at the front of my mind, refusing to be ignored. The medicine had found the file, dusted it off, and dropped it on my desk with a Post-It note saying, "You ready to deal with this?"

Was my failure to connect really an unconscious refusal to be vulnerable? Or had I spent twenty-six years successfully building walls so impenetrable that I could not take them down if I wanted to?

Did I really think my subconscious was going to sit idly by while I sat among perfect strangers, facing down my demons and exposing myself emotionally? Could I trust the medicine enough next time? I thought I had surrendered the first time.

Maybe in a three-day retreat, I could sit in stillness, come to know the faces around me, and explain that I was there to unlearn, to discover what lay beyond the walls I'd constructed.

Maybe this wasn't just about drinking ayahuasca.

Maybe healing wasn't about cracking the shell with brute force.

Maybe it was about softening until the shell gave way on its own.

CHAPTER 23
MUGWORT DREAMS

"Trauma is not what happens to you. Trauma is what happens inside you as a result of what happens to you." –Dr. Gabor Maté

I vowed to spend the next couple of months before the retreat meditating and focusing on what I hoped to accomplish.

I noticed some small shifts in my preferences. I was gravitating toward even fewer news-heavy podcasts, and opting for tea instead of beer.

I also realized how much more time I had now that I wasn't spending several hours in the evenings drinking, and was no longer nursing a headache in the morning. I took that time to journal and read.

I sat in nature without the gnawing anxiety to always be doing something "productive." Instead of fog, there was increasing clarity.

Erin and I took a trip to Colorado with her family, and while wandering through the charming little town of Manitou Springs, I found myself drawn into a "woowoo" shop filled with crystals, tarot decks, and incense. I bought a Turkish chalcedony gemstone—a light blue stone with barely detectable swirls of white. The sign next to it claimed it would absorb negative energy, bring harmony, and encourage inward reflection. A part of me scoffed, *I'm going to need to see some scientific studies to back that up.*

Still, something about the weight of it in my hand felt good. Grounding.

I laughed at myself as I paid for the stone. Who was I?

Despite my long-held interest in homeopathic remedies, and rocks, this was definitely in the realm of things I rolled my eyes at. I'd never given myself permission to explore this territory, just as I hadn't given myself permission to love who I loved until I was in middle age.

I decided to embrace the journey and be open to experiences beyond the walls I'd built for myself or the limits society had spoon-fed me.

I also picked up some Mugwort tea. The label claimed it could induce lucid dreams and enhance spiritual insight. Why not? If nothing else, I figured it would be a good experiment.

That night, after swapping it for my usual Maker's Mark and ginger ale —I was drinking less, but still indulging on vacations, special occasions, and the occasional night out—I had a dream so vivid it took a moment to understand it wasn't real.

In the dream, I was furious—deeply, irrationally furious. A good friend I hadn't seen in years had been at my house and no one had told me. I had missed a chance to reconnect.

As it happened, I had plans to meet up with two old friends while in Colorado. One of the friends had been a dispatcher at SAPD, and she had been on duty the night of the shooting.

Over lunch, she retold the story. I had forgotten she had run one suspect as a man instead of a woman. It was a simple typo, but that mistake had resulted in the system not populating the outstanding murder warrant for one of the three suspects.

When the call came over the radio to send rescue for shots fired, she thought her mistake had cost me my life. Even twenty-five years later, she was emotional retelling it.

She was now running a communications center. She told me, "I still use the story as an example to all my recruits of how important it is to remain vigilant. How a hasty mistake can have enormous consequences."

As she spoke, I saw the weight she had been carrying. A single keystroke had caused her to carry the fear of loss, the fear that she had fatally failed a friend and colleague. For all these years, I had thought I was the only one who carried that night. But the incident had stayed with her, embedding itself as surely as it had in me. We don't have to be in the line of fire for trauma to leave its echoes.

I told her that I loved her and forgave her, even though there was nothing to forgive. I made a mental note to make sure that if we ever held our own workshops, we would not forget our dispatchers. They hear every scream, shot fired, final breath—and yet we never check on them.

How many others were carrying invisible wounds? Firefighters, paramedics, ER nurses, teachers—how many of them had been told to just keep going, shake it off, be strong?

I had always thought of trauma as something that happened to you— something you could point to, something tangible. But it was as much about what you witnessed, what you were powerless to stop. Not a single event, but the stories we carry—the moments that leave cracks, even if we never speak of them.

We all carry wounds we aren't aware of.

CHAPTER 24
HERE WE GO AGAIN

"It is not the mountain we conquer, but ourselves." –Sir Edmund Hillary

---

As I packed for the retreat, doubt crept in. *Are you really going through with this—again?*

Yes. Yes, I am, I told myself. I felt sure that this time I was ready to surrender, connect, and finally experience what so many had described as life-changing and transformative.

In the weeks since my first ceremony, I had asked myself the same questions over and over: *Why am I so drawn to this? What am I really searching for?*

The first time, I had come armed with knowledge, expecting to heal some old wounds, unlock the secrets of the universe, and gain enlightenment.

This time, my approach was more humble. I was ready to receive whatever was meant for me, whether it was gentle guidance or an ugly reckoning.

I would ask for the ability to say goodbye to my father and Amel, and to release the guilt that had held me in its grip for so long. I would ask to soften—to shed the tough exterior I had worn for twenty-six years, and be less suspicious, less hardened, have less of a need for control. I would ask to be more accepting of things I could not change and more forgiving of people who could not.

I would ask to become an easier person to love.

Since 2020, I had become hard to be around. I was deep down political rabbit holes, convinced that I saw the world more clearly than everyone else. My perception that everything was closing in on me made me quick to anger and slow to listen. Add alcohol to the mix, and any conversation could turn into a rant about the state of the world and the corruption I saw everywhere. Where we'd once enjoyed discussing politics and world affairs, Erin slowly withdrew, learning it was better not to engage with me at all.

I had worked hard to clear both my mind and body of toxins. Following *la Dieta* had been easier this time. My mind was clearer; my body, lighter. For the first time in years, I felt peace.

As I neared the church property, a small wooden sign caught my eye: "Pop's Place." I slowed down. Had the sign been there before? If it had, I hadn't noticed it.

Maybe I hadn't been ready to see it. Pop was the nickname we had given my dad later in life. A simple, affectionate shift that fit. Seeing those words now, here, of all places, sent a jolt through me. I took the sign as a good omen.

In my eagerness, I arrived promptly at 1 p.m. The gate was locked, so I rolled down the windows to wait and let the breeze carry away any lingering doubts. With a deep breath, I whispered, "Let's crack this coconut."

Cabin Nine was assigned to me, the same as last time, and I welcomed the familiarity. During check-in, I met other participants on the porch. There was a firefighter from Argentina who was attending his sixth retreat. A woman from Los Angeles had flown across the country to be there. A young woman in her early twenties sat quietly, taking it all in. A jazz musician who had been there before laughed easily with the others.

I begged my subconscious, "Please, let the walls come down."

I chatted with the firefighter about his time in the fire service and his previous ayahuasca experiences. Like Brad, he spoke of the scenes he had processed—victims he had tried to save, moments that had haunted him. He told me that, like me, he had failed to connect the first time.

"It takes time," he assured me.

I was introduced to Rosalia, Inti's mother, who would preside over the ceremonies. I immediately liked her. She had a calm and confident presence. With her flowing gray hair, she had an air of wisdom and strength that put me at ease.

She asked me why I had come. I told her I had worked in law enforcement for twenty-six years and felt jaded and weighed down. I had lost Dad and Amel, and I carried guilt surrounding their deaths.

Rosalia listened intently. Then she asked a question I hadn't prepared for.

"Have you ever been pregnant?"

I hesitated, then answered honestly.

"Yes, twice."

It was something I had spoken about to very few people in my life. My darkest secret, one I had buried deep. I had not considered it might be something I needed to process.

With the interview complete, I re-familiarized myself with the property and reflected on my initial fears about finding a place that operated ethically.

I felt so fortunate to have found Rosalia and Inti. There was no question that they were spiritual leaders in the truest sense of the word. The Centro Espiritualista Luz do Vegetal Church was a living, breathing community built on reverence, stewardship, and a long lineage of wisdom.

They didn't carry themselves like gurus or influencers. There were no flowing robes, flashy credentials, or attempts to dazzle or convince. What they carried was presence, humility, and integrity.

Rosalia had walked this path for decades—long before most people outside the Amazon had heard the word *ayahuasca*. She carried knowledge earned through service and deep devotion. She had been mentored, trained, and trusted—not just with the sacrament, but with people's most vulnerable moments.

In his twenties, Inti spent six years studying with the Lakota people in North America, learning their ways of ceremony and connection to the land. The jungles of South America had shaped him too—both before and after—testing what he'd learned and deepening his understanding. Now in his forties, he carried a presence that didn't come from titles, but from the way he moved through the world: steady, humble, and deeply rooted in what he knew to be sacred.

They expected the same of us. This was not a space for tourists or thrill-seekers. It was a sacred container. A commitment. A sacred trust.

Behind the scenes, the church was structured with care. Every ceremony had protocols. Every participant had support. Consent, confidentiality, and safety were non-negotiable.

This wasn't some pop-up retreat led by someone who drank in Peru for a weekend and came back with a website. It was a responsibility and a calling, and it showed in everything they did. There were safety briefings, panic alarms in every cabin, screening forms, and post-ceremony integration support.

But more than that, there was sacredness. It was present in the land, in the quiet before the ceremony, and in the care with which the sacrament was prepared and offered.

Yes, it was a church. And that word, once so loaded for me, took on a new meaning.

Not rules, punishment, or fear.

But sanctuary, invitation, and veneration.

I hadn't just signed up to drink a powerful medicine. I had stepped into a covenant—with myself, with others, and with something greater.

I took my sleeping bag, blanket, and pillow to the temple. I chose the left side this time, hoping to be among the first to drink the sacrament. The first spot had already been claimed, so I took the next one. I had brought my father's small Japanese dictionary, and I tucked it under my pillow.

I surveyed my space. I had a water bottle and my chalcedony stone. I had my determination.

I returned to my cabin to wait for the ringing of the bell.

CHAPTER 25

THE STORM WITHIN

"No one saves us but ourselves. No one can and no one may. We ourselves must walk the path." –Buddha

---

Dusk settled over the retreat.

I dressed in my white yoga pants and T-shirt and headed to the temple. I no longer felt silly wearing white. Now it felt right: a reminder this was a spiritual journey, to be approached with reverence.

The ceremony opened with a discussion of the program for the weekend and a review of the rules. The importance of staying present, avoiding distractions, and observing the vow of silence that would begin with the start of the ceremony were stressed, along with the importance of not eating anything outside of what was provided by the retreat.

A flicker of guilt crept in. Tucked away in Cabin Nine, I had some snacks, a book, and my phone, which was supposed to have been turned over along with my keys.

I rationalized, *The snacks are on la Dieta. And the book? Just pictures of ayahuasca visions.*

With the administrative matters out of the way, we were ready for the opening prayer. Every ceremony opened and closed with prayer, anchoring us in intention, devotion, and collective stillness.

When my turn for the sacrament came, I approached the altar, kneeled, and accepted the cup from Rosalia. She placed her hand over her heart and whispered softly, "From my heart to yours."

I bowed my head. "I surrender."

Back at my mat, I cupped the chalcedony stone between my palms, chanting softly: "I surrender. I surrender. I surrender."

Unlike the first ceremony, my focus was completely inward. I didn't scan the room or wonder what the other participants were experiencing. I was aware of their presence, but I wasn't bothered by it.

I laid back and let my mind drift—not aimlessly, but going wherever it needed to.

After a while, I felt something: a tingling starting in my abdomen, which spread to my feet. Not unpleasant, but unfamiliar. Next came the unease: a deep stirring in my gut, something shifting, unwinding. I curled myself into a ball, knees to chest, and rocked.

The discomfort became all-consuming.

Outside the temple, I heard a storm gathering. *That's strange*, I thought. The sky had been clear when I entered the temple. However, there was no mistaking it; a storm was coming.

I began thinking about the contraband in my cabin. My hands tightened around something solid: a book.

Wait. This is a book in my hand! My stomach dropped. I was holding Dad's dictionary.

Until now, I hadn't thought of it as a book. I saw it as an extension of him—a tether to something lost. But now, it wasn't only a relic of my father. It was a hidden thing, a thing I had justified keeping, rationalizing it as being exempt.

I haven't surrendered at all. I'm still trying to control everything. Still manipulating the experience, bending the rules while rationalizing my actions. Believing the rules don't apply to me.

I vowed to turn it over in the morning, along with the rest of my prohibited items, and ask for forgiveness.

The storm outside intensified, but something told me this wasn't merely the weather. And then I heard a deafening, piercing, yet familiar sound: an echoing alarm like the "Incoming, incoming, incoming!" warnings in Baghdad and Kabul.

I tried to focus. *What do I do? Seek shelter? Alert the others? Evacuate everyone?*

None of my security protocols fit the situation.

"What am I supposed to do?" I asked the Universe.

No response.

Then it hit me. This wasn't a warning of a rocket attack or a storm. It was inside my head.

My ego, my identity, was on full alert, warning me that everything was about to change. A battle was raging between who I had been and who I was trying to become.

The tension built, coiling through my entire body. My ego wasn't just resisting—it was fighting hard.

I curled into a ball, rocking back and forth. A torrent of emotions surged through me: anguish, pain, fear. There were no thoughts attached to them, no story. Just raw, unfiltered suffering. It felt ancient, like something I had carried for a lifetime.

It must have gone on for some time, because eventually Rosalia came to my side and asked, "Do you need more ayahuasca?"

I looked up at her, barely able to speak. Without thinking, I whispered, "Yes."

Suddenly, I was at the altar, knocking back another cup of the earthy, bitter brew.

No sooner had I returned to my mat than I felt the desperate need to use the bathroom. I barely made it in time to purge from both ends in a release that was also torment.

I couldn't make it the thirty yards to the temple. I collapsed, face down, onto a large bean-bag couch between the bathroom and the temple. One of the volunteer staff placed a blanket over me. I felt comforted, for a moment.

Those waves of emotion slammed into me again and again.

Eventually, I heard music coming from the temple. It was soft and familiar, and I needed to be near it.

Back on my mat, I began rocking again.

The alarm returned, shrill, urgent, and unrelenting. I sensed my ego screaming, "WARNING! WARNING! TURN BACK NOW! THIS IS THE POINT OF NO RETURN!"

My ego was that familiar voice that had always been there, keeping me safe, seeing danger, keeping me alive and sharp. But here, in this sacred place, it wasn't saving me. It was suffocating me. It was refusing to let me release control.

The physical discomfort intensified. *Am I going to die?* I wondered. The pain was unbearable.

And then, after what felt like hours of wrenching, writhing, purging, and fighting with myself at every turn, the physical battle ended.

A single thought rose from the silence.

CHAPTER 26
FORGIVENESS

"If you want to fly, you have to give up the things that weigh you down." –Toni Morrison

---

That thought was of my younger brother, Spencer.

Spencer had passed away in the past year, following an accident on a stolen moped. He was a heroin addict, a criminal. And in the end, a stranger.

I had convinced myself I had no reason to grieve him.

The weight of his loss hit me like a Mack truck. We had once been very close, but over the years, the distance had grown too wide. The lies, theft, and betrayal had built an impenetrable wall between us. When he started conning our mother out of her savings, I lost the last shred of sympathy I had for him.

I sensed the presence of someone else, a woman, who was guiding my thoughts. She showed me I had been wrong to demand an apology from Spencer.

I was the one who needed to ask forgiveness of him. I had abandoned him, forsaken him, and left him alone in the wreckage of his own pain.

I was seized by deep, soul-wracking sobs as I saw how Spencer had struggled after I left for college and Rees left for Korea on his Mormon mission. We had left him behind. Where there had once been a place for him to belong, he stood alone.

I don't know for sure what drove him to take the path he did, but I know he felt alone. Rees and I had left him, right when he needed us most. How had I not seen it before? He had turned to drugs and crime to escape his reality.

And I had written him off.

I had told myself I had no choice. He stole from me and lied to me again and again. He lashed out at me, blaming me for his arrests and calling me a "pig," cursing me as if I had written the criminal complaints against him.

I blocked his number and refused to talk to him—as it turned out, for the rest of his life.

I wailed uncontrollably, saying over and over, "I'm sorry. I'm so sorry."

I saw him again, not as the addict, not as the criminal, but as the little brother I had loved. The little boy in a red sequined vest and tap-dancing shoes. The wild child running up and down the hall, chanting and covered in war paint (mom's lipstick).

And I mourned him. For the first time since he passed, I cried for him.

I cried because I could not deny the fact that if I had taken his calls, maybe I could have made a difference. Maybe I could have been a force for good in his life, rather than another source of pain and regret.

This was the first of the walls I had made too thick, keeping me from connecting with ayahuasca the first time. I had put Spencer's death off-limits.

I had been furious with him for betraying our parents and for turning his two sons against me. When I sat with Rosalia earlier that day, naming the two people I'd lost, I hadn't even thought of Spencer.

I saw the irony—in my own fear of abandonment, how easy it had been for me to write people off and abandon them. I realized I'd abandoned his kids. I had barely spoken to his sons since he died. That had to change, and I vowed to work to repair those damaged relationships.

Now I sensed Dad's presence, waiting patiently. He knew that this grief, this healing, had to come first, and he was content to wait his turn. I told him I would see him tomorrow.

Rosalia went around the temple and asked each participant one by one if they were ready to close the ceremony. Once everyone had returned to this world and was sitting upright on their mats, we gathered in the center for a prayer and a song.

I thanked *La Medicina* for the chance to learn these lessons while there was still time to repair, to begin again with those I had not yet lost.

On my way to the shower, I stopped and looked up at the night sky. The stars were brighter than I had ever seen. There were so many stars, I could barely make out the constellations. Coyotes yipped in the distance, a reminder of home that brought a smile to my face.

After showering, I returned to my cabin, utterly exhausted. I craved sleep, but my mind replayed the night's revelations over and over. I was afraid to forget a single thing, so I got up and journaled, hoping that writing it down would quiet my mind.

Sleep never came, but as dawn crept through the window of Cabin Nine, I knew that this journey was only beginning. I walked to the temple, cleaned my space, and readied myself for the second day.

I could barely stomach the thought of another ceremony, but I wasn't leaving. I wasn't quitting. This was why I had come: to stop running, stop numbing, and stop shutting out the people I couldn't save. To process the past, to heal, and to grow. To learn how to live—really live, not just survive—with the weight of everything I had been carrying.

And, I thought, *Dad is waiting*.

At breakfast, I gathered my contraband and went to find a staff member. "I need to come clean," I admitted, handing it all over: the phone, the snacks, the books.

"I didn't realize dad's dictionary was a book until last night," I apologized.

With eyes full of understanding, they responded, "Thank you for your transparency."

I nodded and turned toward my cabin. The morning air was crisp, the sky pale with first light.

Surely, I thought, *now I have surrendered*.

CHAPTER 27
JOY AND SORROW

The next morning, I walked the grounds, noticing nature in a way I hadn't in a long time. I stopped to watch butterflies zigzagging through the flower gardens, and to listen to the birds singing their melodies. The weather was perfect. I ran my fingers along the plants as I walked the trails, marveling at their power to heal both mind and body. A squirrel paused on a tree trunk, eying me with suspicion. I stood frozen, letting it size me up. Without distractions, it was easy to see and engage with the beauty that surrounded me.

As I neared my cabin, I paused in front of the angel playing the harp. Running my fingers across the wind-chime strings again, I let its tones settle over me. Everything was sharper, clearer, as if my vision had been restored to 20/20.

A little before lunch, I met with Rosalia. She studied me for a moment before smiling. "You don't look like the same woman who arrived yesterday."

I exhaled. I had certainly been through the wringer, and I was exhausted. But there was something else.

A deep, swelling gratitude filled me, not just for Mother Nature, but for the simple fact that I could be here. I felt compelled to write, to pick up trash when I saw it, to move discarded banana peels from the trash to the compost bin.

When I told Rosalia about my experience the night before, she smiled with quiet satisfaction and told me I had done a great job of connecting.

As the day stretched on, I reflected on how difficult the ceremony had been. Could I really do it again—twice more?

During the ceremony, I had heard the woman beside me whispering to herself, "You can do hard things."

As I prepared for the second night—raw, emptied, stripped of illusion —I clung to those words. They reminded me of Erin, who often used that phrase in moments of struggle. I had come here for myself, yes, but I had also come for her, to be a better partner, who didn't carry the weight of the past into every moment of the present.

I decided that would be my mantra for day two: *I can do hard things.*

For the rest of the day, I repeated it to myself, letting it settle into my breath and bones, into the parts of me where doubt still lingered. And as the sun dipped below the horizon, I prayed silently, *Show me what I need to see.*

After taking my turn at the altar, I sat upright on my mat, running my fingers over the chalcedony gemstone, willing my mind to submit. With my ego already knocked down a peg, things got off to a rolling start.

From beneath my mat, a white light rose—soft at first, then radiant, expanding outward like the first breath of dawn. It wrapped around me, weightless, infinite.

From the depths of its glow, two tiny, luminous lotus blossoms unfurled.

I didn't need to be told. I recognized them: the souls of the two pregnancies I had not carried to term.

As the realization took hold, their light flickered, dimmed, and vanished into the void.

A sharp cramping sensation coiled through my abdomen, the weight of sorrow pressing into me like an anchor. The grief I had buried long ago surfaced, raw and undeniable.

I made my way to the bathroom, where I cried out as a flood of emotion poured out of me, literally and figuratively.

On the way back to the temple, I could only make it as far as the fire pit. I collapsed into a chair, purging into the grass. Rosalia came to my side with a bucket. I stumbled to the beanbag couch and curled into a ball as waves of cramping and purging overtook me.

I mourned them. Not in the way I had thought of them before—not as distant echoes or quiet regrets left unspoken. I mourned them as genuine pieces of me. With each sob that tore through my body, something loosened—grief unraveling from the depths of my being.

I had spent so many years holding it all in. Now, as I let it go, I found forgiveness in the release.

As the pain in my body subsided, a third lotus blossom appeared. I recognized it instantly as the baby Erin had lost when we had tried to conceive in Hermosillo. For the first time, I saw it as our baby, realizing finally that I had never allowed myself to grieve that loss or accept it as my own.

Now, the pain of the loss washed over me, and I bore the weight of Erin's sorrow and my own.

The woman to my right sobbed softly. I could feel sorrow emanating from her too.

And then—faces. One after another, they emerged from the darkness.

In addition to my own sorrow, and Erin's sorrow, I began to feel the sorrow of others.

Victims whose cases had crossed my desk. Strangers whose grief and pain I had borne witness to. People whose pain had lodged itself within me, taking root in the hidden spaces of my soul.

As it always has, my body struggled to breathe when faced with such pain.

First was the terminally ill woman I'd met as a young police officer. She had threatened suicide, in so much pain from her illness that she couldn't bear to go on. I had befriended her and checked in on her from time to time on my patrols, but I could do very little to help her.

I felt Amel's torment when Hazim was taken, her anguish as she negotiated the ransom, her fear when she, too, was taken.

I saw the Kurdish father at Saddam Hussein's trial, recounting the loss of his wife and five children during the chemical attacks. I saw him remove his shirt to show the court his scars from the burns that would never fully heal. I saw Saddam sitting at the front of the courtroom, unmoved.

I saw the young Ugandan rebel leader who came to the embassy seeking asylum. Like many young people, she had been kidnapped as a child by Joseph Kony's men and turned into a soldier. She had been horribly abused before making her way up in the ranks to become a very hard woman. At substantial risk to herself, she wanted to give information on his whereabouts in exchange for safe passage to the United States. I spent hours taking down her story. Beneath the tough exterior, I saw the scared little girl who had once been taken from her home by force.

I saw the five-year-old girl I'd carried through the airport in El Salvador, her pain as she kicked my ribs and screamed at me, wailing with a terror that covered me like a wet blanket.

I saw the young prostitute from a case I'd worked while in internal affairs. She was barely eighteen years old, picked up on the street of a third-world country by a U.S. diplomat, expecting food and money for sex. She was drugged and brutalized instead.

I saw my Afghan staff, who had trusted their American bosses to protect them if things went sideways; their fear and sense of betrayal as they waited in hiding, wondering if they had been forgotten, wondering if they would be left behind and subjected to retaliation by the Taliban for working with the United States government.

Finally, I saw my father. I saw the joy leave him as he was consumed by guilt—the unbearable weight of having taken the life of a highway worker in a horrible traffic accident. His deep sadness pressed down on me, suffocating me.

It all crashed down on me. I couldn't breathe.

I had carried all their pain for years without recognizing it.

I reached for my bucket as the purge came in wave after wave of violent, gut-wrenching convulsions. This wasn't the contents of my stomach emptying; it was grief, sorrow, and guilt, spilling out of me in torrents: every cry I had swallowed, every pain I had carried. Every wound I had refused to look at was working its way up from the depths of my soul.

When the waves subsided, I collapsed onto my mat, drenched in exhaustion.

The deafening alarm tone from the night before rang out again. This time, I understood what it was: my ego trying desperately to draw a line in the sand.

I heard a woman's voice in my head, motherly, loving, and gentle.

I wondered, *Are you God? The Universe? Mother Nature? Mother Ayahuasca? All of them?*

She whispered, "Empathy is good. You cannot carry only sorrow though. It will consume you."

Her presence, warm and steady, washed away all the pain that had filled me.

"There must be balance," She continued. "For every grief you hold, you must hold joy. Seek it. Embrace it. Let it fill you as fully as pain has."

The white light returned, but not from underneath my mat. It was glowing from within me. I placed my hands over my heart, feeling its warmth.

"This is yours to protect. To nourish. To share."

I thought of people in my life who were celebrating proud moments: becoming grandparents, kids joining the Marines, kids going to, or graduating, college.

I saw the night sky through the screened wall of the temple. Suddenly, I was soaring through the galaxy.

I heard my plants speaking to me. Some of them told me they needed more sun. Others whispered they were crowded and wished to be spread out. I wondered if plants communicated in Spanish, realizing with a smile that all the dialogue in my head was in Spanish—a language I had studied, yet struggled to speak.

I understood that the purpose of life is to find joy, and joy comes from the simplest things: plants, dogs, family, love.

From the front of the temple, I heard panting. I looked over and saw Chief, my scruffy Ugandan street dog, standing in the doorway.

He ran toward me, and I threw my arms around his skinny neck, burying my face in his fur. I heard his adorable little whimper, the one he made when I came home after a long trip.

Then, all the dogs I had lost throughout my life appeared: Patches. Teddy. Bam Bam. Dozer. Chewy. Boo. They ran to me, tails wagging, jumping and playing in a field of soft, white light.

In the distance, figures emerged. At first shadows, then faces, familiar and beloved.

My dad. My grandmother. Spencer.

They stood before me, smiling. Whole. Radiant. Free. There was no sadness in their eyes. No pain. No regret.

Only love.

The voice whispered. "There is no reason to fear death. There is only joy after this life. No sadness. No guilt. No pain. Only joy."

I felt my dad's love. I saw myself through his eyes. I was still his happy, giggling daughter. I was still Snickers, and I always would be.

As Rosalia closed the ceremony, I placed my hand over my heart and whispered a prayer of gratitude to Mother Ayahuasca for bringing me back to the light.

I showered, returned to my cabin, and collapsed into bed. Again, sleep did not come, but I was at peace.

I was looking forward to day three.

CHAPTER 28
SURRENDER

"When you walk on the way, the way appears." –Rumi

In the morning, I met with Rosalia. The moment she saw me, her expression softened. Her eyes brimmed with something between awe, and what seemed like recognition.

"You no longer have the face of a woman," she said. "You have the face of a child."

I told her about the light I had seen coming from within me, and my desire to share it. She grinned and nodded knowingly.

I spent the rest of the day reflecting on the first two ceremonies.

Twenty-six years ago, I had sworn to be a force for good in the world—to wear the badge with integrity, to serve with compassion. I had done my best to live up to that, but somewhere along the way, shadows crept in.

The hardening came slowly: a closed door here, a disappointment there. The things I'd seen and experienced had layered over me like scar tissue, thick and numbing, until one day, I could no longer feel the warmth beneath.

I had told myself I was protecting myself, that walking away from those who hurt me was survival. I wasn't abandoning them; I was setting boundaries.

One by one, I had let them go—Spencer, my niece Danni, and my two nephews. I had built walls between myself and my mother, convinced they were necessary. Even Erin, the one person I had promised never to shut out, had commented on the weight of my distance.

With every damaged relationship, I lost another part of myself.

Mother Ayahuasca had gone in and cut away the scar tissue, breaking it loose, so it could be purged from my body. Now, I could finally see that joy and sorrow are balancing forces. Neither can exist without the other.

I looked in the mirror, searching for any visible change in my appearance. I wondered if Erin would see a change.

I walked the grounds, enjoying the stillness and remembering the quote about the seed that must crack open to achieve its fullest expression.

My shell had cracked.

My insides had come out.

Now it was time to find out if I was ready to take root.

I walked to the temple, steady, unburdened in white. When Rosalia extended the cup, I accepted it without resistance. As the warmth spread through my body, the woman's voice returned, calm and unwavering: "You will drink another cup tonight."

It's too soon, I thought. *There's still time.*

She was patient, amused even. "I'm just letting you know. Prepare yourself."

I exhaled. *Not yet*, I bargained. *Not yet.*

I could sense Mother Ayahuasca digging through my mind, searching for the next place that needed healing. It did not take Her long to find it: the fear I had carried since birth. The fear of being unwanted, rejected.

I saw myself in the womb of a mother who knew she could not care for me. I thought of my adopted mother who had wanted children, but struggled to be nurturing.

It wasn't rejection or cruelty. It was simply her way of being. For the first time, I did not meet that truth with resentment. I met it with gratitude. I finally understood that she had done the best she could. There was no need to be angry.

I was grateful for my birth mother—for choosing life, for choosing adoption over the alternative, even as a young, unmarried college student.

She had more courage than I had when I found myself in that position.

My thoughts turned to Erin. I saw how I had been drawn to her because she made me feel safe, wanted, nurtured.

I saw that I had been allowing us to grow apart. My fear of abandonment and rejection, my need for connection, had clouded my ability to see that we were already deeply connected.

Mother Ayahuasca's voice returned, gentle as the wind through the trees. "You are loved. You are enough."

And suddenly I knew. She had always been with me—whispering in the rustling leaves, in the sun on my face, the grass beneath my bare feet. It had always been Her. Mother Nature. God. She had been calling me home.

I was overwhelmed with love—for myself. I ran my fingers through my hair, feeling the softness of my curls. I caressed my face, wrapped my arms around myself in a loving embrace.

I heard Rosalia singing and thought, "She has the voice of an angel." Although she was singing in Spanish, and I could not understand all the words, I knew she was speaking of healing the mind and soul.

A steady stream of soft, nonsensical sounds and phrases spilled from my lips. "Awe...some. Woo...saa. Oh...yeah."

I was aware the temple was silent that night, but I could not lie quietly.

I saw myself from above, bathed in pure white light, wrapped in my own arms. My dad approached from behind me and wrapped his arms around mine. "I love you and always will," he said.

I saw how I had shunned laughter and joy. From my dad's booming laugh that embarrassed me as a teenager, that I would now give anything to hear again; to the ring-tone Amel had chosen for the kidnappers; laughter had become a source of pain when it should have been a pathway to joy.

I began to giggle—to snicker.

From across the temple, I heard the jazz musician belching. Deep, gleeful, childlike belches. It made me laugh harder. It wasn't just funny, it was a bridge back to joy. Laughter overtook me, shaking loose something buried too long.

I saw my dad ascending toward a bright ball of light. I could finally see him as the man I knew and loved before the spark left him. He was joyful and at peace. I knew, without a doubt, that he would always be with me.

Ten years before, I had sat beside my father, watching his chest rise and fall through the rhythm of machines, hoping he'd wake up, hoping I would not have to make an impossible decision. I played his favorite songs by The Beatles, hoping the music he loved might bring him back. He never regained consciousness.

I hadn't listened to The Beatles since that night. Even a few bars of their music triggered a grief so piercing, I'd turn it off before the first verse ended.

Now I could finally let him go, knowing that he remained in the laughter, the stars, and the music he loved.

"Don't try so hard to feel connected to your loved ones," my guide told me. "You are already connected."

I understood then that everything is connected—made of the same energy. No one thing is better or worse than another. It's all moving through the world in different forms, on different frequencies, but fundamentally the same.

She told me I needed to understand frequencies and learn how to tune in. I was on board—I wanted to understand what frequency plants operated on, to hear what they had to say.

She assured me that if I took more sacrament, She would show me everything. She would take me to the next level. But my body clenched in rebellion. I couldn't move toward the altar. I tried to negotiate, to stall.

Her voice sharpened. "DO IT NOW."

I dug in my heels. Not yet.

Another battle erupted deep within. My ego, bruised but unrelenting, still clung to control.

Mother Ayahuasca showed me all the ways I was weak, all the ways I was a hypocrite: I claimed I had dedicated my life to protecting others, yet I hadn't had the courage to save two innocent lives when I had the chance. I claimed I cut toxic people out of my life out of self-respect, yet I didn't respect myself enough to eat properly, exercise, or stop drinking. I claimed I wanted the secrets of the universe revealed to me, yet when the door was opened, I hesitated to walk through it.

"HOW BADLY DO YOU WANT IT?" Mother Ayahuasca demanded.

She told me I had to do the work. Mental anguish consumed me. I moaned, "No, no, no, no, no." The battle went on and on. She kept telling me to drink, and my mind and body kept refusing.

I saw staff collecting the cups from the railing. My chance had slipped away.

I was weak.

I knew I would regret it. Shame burned through me. Desperate, I called out to Rosalia, "Is it too late for more sacrament?"

She had offered me more earlier, saying, "Come when you are ready."

"You want more ayahuasca?" she asked.

My soul whispered yes, as my mind screamed no. She motioned for me to come to the altar, and I stumbled forward. My cup was gone, but she handed me a small one, maybe a third of the size.

"From my heart to yours," she said as she handed me the tiny cup.

Tears welled up and spilled over as I took the little cup between my fingers. I hung my head and whispered, "It's so hard." I was kneeling before the altar, frozen. The cup trembled in my hand. Long seconds passed. I lifted the cup to my lips, and my whole body resisted. I fought through the resistance and swallowed.

I collapsed on all fours, completely spent. I crawled on my hands and knees through the soft sand and slumped, face down, halfway onto my mat.

Violent purging overtook me. I couldn't swallow. My throat was closing. I gasped for air. Nothing came.

"Don't fight it," the voice implored. "You must die before you can be reborn."

The mental and physical anguish was unbearable.

I struggled against it until I had no fight left. Finally, I stopped trying to breathe.

My heart stopped. Just for a fraction of a second: the space between life and death, between fear and release.

Panic surged—then vanished. Air flooded my lungs. My body convulsed with a gasp, a desperate inhale of life itself.

A chuckle echoed through the void. "Congratulations. Your reward is freedom."

Tears spilled down my face. I laughed, not from relief, but from the pure, unshackled joy of being alive. I reached toward the sky, fingers spread wide, swaying to the music.

I heard a beautiful bell ringing. It was the singing bowls.

But it was also the alarm tone from the past two nights. Only this time, the frequency didn't hurt my ears. This time, it sounded like heaven.

It really was all about frequency, and I was finally tuning in.

As the ceremony concluded, the participants formed a circle around the candles and held hands. Someone began laughing. Soon everyone was laughing. Deep, belly-shaking laughter like Buddha. Like children. Like souls free of burdens.

I looked around the circle at the faces glowing in the candlelight. I saw love, joy, acceptance, and friendship.

We had not spoken a single word to each other in three days, yet we had shared our deepest pain. We had grieved and healed together. We were connected.

I turned to the woman beside me. She wrapped me in a tight embrace. "I love you," she whispered, kissing my cheek.

The vow of silence was over. We were invited to enjoy a feast that had been prepared, and to sit by the bonfire.

As I sat by the fire watching the flames dance, I could feel the ayahuasca still working through me. I didn't feel ready to join the group, so I returned to my cabin. I lay in bed, rocking gently. Breath and sound moved through me—moans, sighs, groans—years of suppressed grief, anger, and fear finding release.

Mother Ayahuasca was inside me, working like a surgeon, cutting away the scar tissue, peeling away the calluses of the years spent maintaining a stoic, professional exterior.

I now understood why COVID had shaken me so deeply. It wasn't just the policies; it was what they revealed about me. Being told to comply silently and without question struck an ancient nerve.

A lifetime of swallowing emotion, a career of compartmentalizing truth, were all rising to the surface.

I saw the Grim Reaper hovering above me, cloaked in black. "Congratulations, your ego is now dead," my guide announced. I had built an identity around control and survival, and I felt it lift away, like a weight releasing from my bones. I knew there was still work to do, but I felt freer than I had in a long time.

She told me She had nothing left to show me that night. She had opened the door in my mind. Now it was up to me to stay on the right frequency. I thanked Her for everything—for testing, breaking, and rebuilding me.

Around 1:30 a.m. I made my way to the bonfire. The group welcomed me warmly. Someone grinned and said, "There she is. The Eagle has landed."

As I sat by the fire, I couldn't shake the feeling every single person there was supposed to be there at that exact moment in time. In ways I couldn't fully comprehend, we had all been called to that place, that weekend, and each other.

I wondered if anything I had done—any word I had spoken, or energy I had given—had helped them as much as they had helped me.

I thanked the firefighter whose panting by the door brought Chief to me. I had finally found closure with his unexplained disappearance.

I thanked Rosalia for her angelic voice, allowing me to find my way through the pain and anguish.

I thanked the jazz musician for his wild belches that ushered laughter back into my life.

I thanked the woman whose mantra, "I can do hard things," brought Erin's love and support to me as I faced my demons.

Finally, I thanked the woman on the other side of me whose gentle sobbing had helped me realize that with pain there must also be joy.

I hugged Inti and told him how grateful I was for the church.

The next morning, I stepped into the temple to collect my things. As my feet sank into the soft sand, I knew that the real work was yet to come. Ayahuasca had opened the door. Now I had to walk through it.

I had been broken open, but any lasting change would depend on what I did next.

PART FOUR
GRAFTING NEW BRANCHES

CHAPTER 29
COLLATERAL MEMORIES

In the days and weeks following the retreat, my mind began the process of integration. Old memories continued to surface—things I hadn't let myself look at. Iraq was one of them.

I arrived in Baghdad for a 45-day assignment in late 2004, fresh out of training and invincible, ready to tackle any challenge that came my way.

Along with four other eager DS agents, I took commercial air to Kuwait, then traveled under the cover of darkness into Baghdad International Airport (BIAP) on a C-130. The low hum and the sickening tilt as the pilot took evasive action before dropping onto the tarmac were our reminder: we were entering a war zone.

The short drive from BIAP to Saddam's former palace, now home to the U.S. Embassy, was too dangerous, so we boarded Blackhawk helicopters.

I was assigned to the Tactical Operations Center. Part of my duties involved taking an approved access list to the checkpoints early each morning. The checkpoints were staffed by Nepalese guards, who were polite and precise, trained in the British tradition. They greeted me with a bright, "Hello, sir!" I didn't take offense. I knew their intent was to show respect. Some called me "sir-ma'am," which I found especially endearing.

I'd return their greeting with "Namaste" and tried to learn their names. I grew fond of Ranja, who worked the service entrance. He had a mischievous sparkle I appreciated. One morning, I stepped inside the checkpoint and heard a muffled clucking. "What is that?" I asked.

Ranja grinned and pointed to a bag near the wall. "Chicken," he confided proudly. Sure enough, the bag rustled and clucked again.

"Why is there a chicken inside the checkpoint?" I inquired, raising an eyebrow.

"I eat it," he replied, grinning from ear to ear.

It became a running joke. "More chickens today?" I'd ask. "No chicken today," he'd reply, shaking his head.

Then came the rocket strike.

A volley of rounds hit the compound—one landing directly on the tents the Nepalese guards were housed in. Four were killed instantly.

The fire spread quickly, destroying bunks, uniforms, everything. Each tent housed up to fifty Nepalese guards. Had it been night, the death toll would have been far worse.

When I made my rounds the next morning, the air was heavy. The guards' usual smiles were gone. Some sat slumped against walls, red-eyed or asleep. I let them be. As long as one was alert, I moved on.

By the time I reached the service checkpoint, I was holding my breath.

Had Ranja survived? When I stepped inside and saw him standing there, I exhaled.

"Many at internet café," he said sadly. "Or doing laundry. Very lucky."

"I'm glad you're safe," I replied.

Before I left, I told him, "I hope there are no rockets today."

"Yes," he smiled sadly, "no rockets today."

I remember that day not for the destruction, but for the silence and the quiet dignity. For Ranja's smile, still warm in the shadow of loss.

When that assignment was over, the same group of five DS agents spent another night in Kuwait. We went to TGI Friday's for dinner. As we walked through the parking lot, fireworks exploded in the distance —not a car bomb detonating or a rocket impact. We all flinched and froze. I'm still waiting for the day I can hear fireworks and not feel the urge to dive for cover.

When I returned to Iraq for a one-year assignment in 2006, the Green Zone was struck by nearly 365 rockets, many of them landing on the embassy compound. Not one a day, but in clusters—volleys that often came in waves. The second round was frequently timed to catch first responders. In the early days, we responded anyway.

Sometimes, we got a few seconds of warning. A loudspeaker would blare, "Incoming, incoming, incoming!"

At first, I dove for the nearest bunker. Later, I got complacent.

One night, an Iraqi military ammo depot nearby was hit by insurgents. The ordnance inside cooked off—booming like thunder, striking randomly around the city, inside the Green Zone. There was nothing to do but wait it out.

I took two Benadryl, put on my Kevlar helmet, covered myself with a Kevlar blanket, and laid down beside the sandbagged wall of my "hooch." When I woke up, the explosions had stopped. I seemed none the worse for wear, save for a stiff neck from having slept in my helmet.

Another time, a co-worker and I were in an outbuilding, preparing to interview an employee suspected of stealing U.S. property. His attorney was on speaker-phone from D.C. We had barely gotten started when a rocket hit outside, rattling the windows—hard.

We dove under the desks. Silence followed, heavy and thick.

A voice crackled through the speaker: "Guys? What's happening?"

My colleague reached out from under the desk and hit disconnect, saying, "We're getting rocketed. We'll call you back."

We threw on our medical response kits and ran outside. More rockets followed. We ducked into a bunker and waited it out. Later we laughed about what that attorney must have thought.

Midway through the tour, I developed a sharp pain in my right ear. The med unit found no infection, but the pain got worse in the afternoons—sometimes so bad I couldn't function. I also battled a chronic cough for most of the tour.

Volunteering at our improvised watering hole became my escape. The "Lock & Load"—a makeshift bar DS agents had rigged together in the courtyard of a cluster of outbuildings—was offices by day and bar by night, complete with a counter, a frozen drink machine, and the occasional batch of homemade brew. I loved the small jolt of adrenaline that came with beer runs inside the Green Zone and found real pleasure in working behind the bar, which was always packed. It was a place to decompress and feel briefly normal. Drinking also helped to numb the stabbing pain in my jaw and ear.

As the new U.S. Embassy neared completion, efforts were made to "normalize" operations—to transform the Wild West chaos into something that resembled a "real" embassy. Those in charge of normalizing said we couldn't sell alcohol, so we sold punch cards that could be traded for drinks. When that no longer worked, we declared it a private party, locked the gate, and kept serving.

It was a bizarre tour.

"Normal" was seldom achieved and often actively resisted. A plate dropped on the floor sent people running for the bunkers, but an explosion that shook the ground under your feet barely caused anyone to look up.

After twelve months of mayhem and mortar fire, I wanted somewhere very different: untamed, but relatively safe. So I accepted an onward assignment in Kampala, Uganda.

It was like stepping into another world. One week I was dodging rocket warnings; the next, I was watching boda-bodas weave through traffic. After Iraq's constant tension, Uganda felt almost disorienting: quieter, softer, but in its own way, just as complex.

Instead of a connex-box for housing, I had a two-story house on Kololo Hill. It should have felt like a reward, a reprieve from sandbags and ear-piercing alarms. Instead it was hollow and vast.

In Baghdad, I had rarely slept, unless I'd numbed myself with alcohol or antihistamines. It didn't take much to jolt me upright. My first night in that massive house, I heard the front door handle jiggle. Then I heard it again—a soft rattle, unmistakable.

I didn't have a firearm. I didn't have my household effects yet. My brain took inventory of my resources: hairspray, cellphone, a couple of books.

I crept downstairs, hairspray in hand, and found a man in a uniform and a ball cap standing at the front door.

He mumbled something non-threatening as I came into view. He was a member of the embassy guard force conducting nightly residence checks. No one had told him the house was now occupied.

My heart was still pounding even after he apologized profusely.

Navigating traffic in Kampala—a city where "personal space" didn't exist on the roads—was a tense ordeal. After a year in Baghdad, where any vehicle that got too close was treated as a potential threat, the constant crowding of cars and motorbikes made me uneasy.

I used to think I came back untouched. Ayahuasca allowed me to see that I had come back numb. She didn't just unearth the memories, She let me feel them, fully and without fear.

CHAPTER 30
THE BODY REMEMBERS

"The body keeps the score." –Bessel van der Kolk

As I learned to approach life from a more centered place, I came to appreciate something I'd resisted for a long time: we all have limits. And eventually, "powering through" stops working. There's a fine line between resilience and denial—between carrying on, and coming apart.

I had seen it more than once in my career. People who broke, not in a single dramatic moment, but slowly, quietly, with a thousand micro-fractures, until something finally gave way.

During my time working in roles related to personal accountability, we routinely received cases involving individuals who, on paper, had committed misconduct. But the deeper truth was harder to categorize. It wasn't criminal behavior. It was collapse. People unraveling under pressure that had gone unspoken and unmet for far too long.

One officer began singing in the streets outside the embassy, dancing through the security checkpoints, and laughing uncontrollably during formal meetings. Another sent rambling, paranoid emails to colleagues. One sought asylum in another country, convinced "they" were after him. I had a boss who had once been capable and respected. A year of unrelenting volatility wore him down to the point that he wandered the embassy at night in his boxers and slept in his office, no longer feeling safe enough to leave the building.

From where I sat, these public servants did not appear to be security risks. They were human beings in pain. I saw a system that wasn't equipped to respond to that kind of suffering, so it was labeled misconduct and routed into investigative channels. But these people didn't need investigation—they needed someone to say, "I see you."

After arriving in Uganda, I wasn't sleeping. My jaw ached constantly and the pain radiated into my ear. In between the assignments to Iraq and Uganda, an ENT finally named the issue: Temporomandibular Joint disorder—TMJ. I was grinding my teeth at night so hard the muscles in my jaw seized up. He gave me muscle relaxers, which helped —for a while.

In the years that followed, I spent a small fortune adjusting my bite and having custom night guards made. But I couldn't escape the question: what was causing me to clench my teeth? Like the stress-induced asthma I developed earlier in my lifer, no one could pinpoint a cause. And there was no clear or approved treatment.

When I first arrived in Kampala, I started taking Mefloquine, the standard anti-malarial. Shortly after, I noticed my moods spiraling and began having nightmares.

Is this the Mefloquine? I wondered. *Or something else?*

PTSD wasn't a label that applied to me. That was for combat vets, people who stormed beaches. Not people like me. I hadn't earned that diagnosis.

But trauma doesn't care whether you've earned it. It doesn't check your résumé or weigh your valor. It waits. And if you don't face it, eventually, it will face you.

I spoke with the med unit, and we agreed I'd take a "medication vacation." The acute symptoms faded, but the unease didn't. I couldn't shake the feeling that something in me had shifted off-center, and stayed there.

I knew part of it was Amel. There's no checkbox for guilt. No standard form for "I wish I could have done more."

I was afraid to seek counseling, which could trigger a flag on my security clearance. In our world, marriage counseling was fine, grief counseling acceptable. But depression? Anxiety? Emotional instability? Those could be grounds for a fitness-for-duty review.

I spoke to someone, once, under the banner of grief. Through heavy sobs, I told him about Amel, about the guilt I carried. He listened quietly, then declared, "You're experiencing survivor's guilt." It was the first time I'd heard the phrase. Now that it had a name, I filed it away. Problem identified; move on.

Ten years later, I stopped in London on my way home from a work trip to Kenya. I took an Uber out to the countryside, to the cemetery where Amel and Hazim were buried. I wandered among the headstones until I found theirs.

The stone was dirty, the lettering difficult to make out. I found some paper towels in a nearby dumpster and cleaned it with the water from my water bottle.

Then I sat, and cried, and asked for forgiveness.

Afterward, I found a pub and drank. It wasn't closure, but it was the closest I had come.

Years later, I worked with another DS agent to have Amel's name added to the official memorial honoring FSNIs killed in the line of duty. It still wasn't closure.

Maybe the medicine was finally bringing me that.

CHAPTER 31

I'M SELF-TAUGHT

"When you want something, all the universe conspires in helping you to achieve it." –Paulo Coelho, *The Alchemist*

In the Ozarks, the work of integrating Mother Ayahuasca's lessons into my life and worldview continued as I threw myself into a construction project.

At first, doing the work myself was about saving money. Soon, I discovered that I also loved the work. There was something grounding, almost meditative, about building with my own hands. I wasn't only learning new skills—I was also pushing past my limits in new ways.

I've never been a fan of heights, but wiring the building meant working up on scaffolding, balancing while threading electrical wire through ceiling joists, with arms raised above my head for hours.

With the help of a dear friend and former sergeant at SAPD, who was also retired, we pulled over four thousand feet of wire throughout the building. It was exhausting, physically demanding work that left my shoulders burning, hands cramping, and patience wearing thin. It tested my endurance and willingness to keep going when every muscle begged me to quit. Every challenge conquered made the vision feel more real—board by board, wire by wire.

I was fortunate to have another friend who knew construction well, and was willing to teach and help me with the building. He was patient —until he wasn't.

One day, after I completely botched something, he turned to me, clearly annoyed, and asked, "Where the hell did you learn to do it that way?"

I smiled and shrugged. "I'm self-taught."

He shook his head as he laughed despite himself, muttered something under his breath, and showed me the right way to do it. I knew I wasn't making his life easier, but every mistake taught me something, and I was determined to keep learning.

I gained a whole new appreciation for the trades. The skill, craftsmanship, and sheer physical endurance it required humbled me. My career had been physically demanding, but in fits and starts, usually during training more than the day-to-day. Construction was often physically demanding for hours and hours, day after day.

It was rewarding to step back, covered in sawdust or drywall dust, and see something taking shape. For years, I had been a protector of people and institutions. Now, I was learning to be a protector, and creator, of something else: space. Space for things like healing, reconnection, or transformation.

Along the way, the Universe sent little winks of encouragement. I scoured Facebook Marketplace for materials—windows, re-bar, surplus supplies from other projects—and kept manifesting what I needed, like flooring in the perfect amount, and tools and supplies at just the right time. Even when I sold my beloved FJ40 that I'd brought back from El Salvador, the sale amount came almost exactly to what I needed to buy a tractor. These weren't coincidences; they felt like confirmations from the Universe that I was on the right track.

Bit by bit, the vision was becoming real. Not in one grand moment, but through a thousand minor acts of effort, trust, and letting go. I was building a new way of being, one rooted in patience, presence, and faith that what was meant for me would find me, as long as I kept showing up, tools in hand, heart open. Construction became almost a form of meditation, teaching me patience.

My spiritual practice was taking shape too. Each morning, I would journal, read, and meditate before pouring a cup of coffee, greeting the sun, and walking the property with the dogs. Life carried on much the same, but small changes kept quietly revealing themselves.

I was more patient with others, and myself. Things that once would have frustrated me just—didn't. I wasn't in a blissed-out haze, but there was an ease and lightness which hadn't been there before. I was also less afraid. Not recklessly, but in the sense that the future no longer seemed so heavy. I didn't need to have all the answers or control every outcome. That realization alone was freeing.

Still, I knew I wasn't done. Ayahuasca had shown me lost pieces of myself, but I could feel deeper layers still buried, things I hadn't yet faced. Inside the coconut, there was an onion, and it still had layers to peel.

For the most part, I was able to quickly process and understand what I saw in ceremony. I remember mentioning this to Rosalia, and from her response, I wondered if that was not the norm.

Still, there were moments that left me puzzled. Once, I saw a peyote cactus. I wasn't sure if it was an invitation to explore that plant medicine, to contemplate Indigenous traditions in modern culture, or something else entirely.

Another night I saw a series of lottery numbers riding the sound waves out through the cupola, followed by a brilliant flash of light. Fireworks and confetti rained down. The question, "What would you do if you won?" led to images of a retreat in the Ozarks—horses, hiking trails, therapy dogs, yoga, meditation. Maybe Inti would consider facilitating ceremonies from time to time. The words looped in my mind: Plants, animals, people. Repair, restore, renew. I let myself dream of dedicating it all to others.

The most confusing image I received was a three-dimensional geometric shape—a cube with a suspended ball in the center, intersected by lines. I tried to find it online. The closest match was the sacred geometry symbol for the Tree of Life or a Kabbalistic diagram, but nothing was exact. That led me to briefly explore Kabbalah teachings, some of which resonated deeply; some, not as much.

Almost a year later, I would see the shape again, in Brussels, Belgium, while visiting the 1958 World's Fair exhibit known as the Atomium. The structure stands over 330 feet high, an atom magnified 165 billion times. I stood beneath it, head tilted back, awed by its symmetry and light. In that moment, I felt sure I was meant to understand something simple and vast: everything is made of atoms. We are, quite literally, all the same.

A friend of mine who follows Toltec wisdom once cautioned me, "Don't try to cram something sacred into a box so it makes sense." His words stayed with me—a reminder to resist the urge to explain every mystery. Some mysteries reveal themselves in days or weeks. Others take months—or a lifetime.

I began to wonder what layers I still had to peel back, and what they would reveal. Was I brave enough to let it all surface? Could I ever reach a place where fear and doubt no longer had a grip on me? The call to return didn't take long. I lined up the retreat schedule with the construction schedule and booked another three-day retreat.

At the close of the last retreat, Inti had mentioned that ayahuasca resets you, saying, "You might find your preferences change—music, food, alcohol, people, even the places you want to be. You're vibrating at a higher frequency now."

He had been right—especially regarding alcohol. But that shift didn't happen overnight.

Not long after my first retreat, Erin and I visited Key West and booked a sunset kayaking tour. We could tell that the guide, Kevin, was exactly the kind of character Key West specializes in—barefoot, tan lines, and an easy smile that said he'd long since stopped caring about clocks or careers. As if that were not evidence enough, he texted and told us to meet him at the bar. Not the dock, the bar.

I'd already had a couple of gin and tonics by the time he pulled up a stool and ordered his own. By the time we pushed our kayaks into the water, I was half-lit and "leaning in."

I was reading *The Celestine Prophecy* by James Redfield, and making a conscious effort to "Lean In" to conversations with strangers, trusting that if the Universe put someone in front of me, there was something to learn.

We hadn't left the harbor before "Kayak Kevin" and I were deep into an animated conversation about psychedelics, my new favorite subject. I caught Erin's eye, blue as the water beneath us. She gave me that half-smile of hers, the one that says, *You're a little over the top, and I'm watching.*

At some point Kevin mentioned a bar you could paddle right up to. That sounded like the best idea I'd ever heard, so we did it. We tied off the kayaks, ordered another round, and completely missed the sunset—and the tour altogether, really. We abandoned the kayaks and walked—well, Erin walked; I stumbled—along the pier in the dark back to our starting point, ending the night the same way we started: at the bar.

The next day, as I nursed a hangover well into the afternoon, Erin suggested with a smile, "Maybe learn to lean in, but not fall out."

That night turned out to be the last time I overindulged. In the months that followed, the desire to unwind by drinking simply disappeared. It felt empty and hollow. I worried that the shift would lead to tension with Erin—our social life had long revolved around shared drinks.

At one retreat, I spoke to Rosalia about my concerns. "What if I grow—and she doesn't?"

Rosalia didn't sugarcoat it. "That can happen. But it's no reason not to grow. If two people become less compatible when only one grows, that is just the way it is."

I knew she was right. Stopping my spiritual journey out of fear was not an answer. And in my heart, I knew Erin was also growing. Her methods were more conventional, but she was evolving in her own time.

While I had long since distanced myself from organized religion and referred to myself as a "recovering Mormon," Erin remained a private Catholic. She talked little about it, but every night, she prayed, hands folded, silently speaking to God. At family gatherings, she did the motions with everyone else while I stood beside her awkwardly, annoyed by what I perceived as gestures without meaning. Now the tables had turned. I was the one praying, asking for guidance, and following a calling I didn't fully understand.

Erin was my ballast—the one who grounded me, keeping me from drifting too far, too fast. She trusted structure: rules, traditions, and the quiet lines that hold things together. I was drawn instead to testing boundaries, questioning the rules, and asking whether they still made sense. Her steadiness tempers my risk; my questioning stretches her certainty. Between the two, we find balance.

CHAPTER 32
THE BACK PORCH

"We are all just walking each other home." –Ram Dass

The gate was open. I drove in, parked, and carried my sleeping bag to the temple, instinctively claiming my spot. A small group had already gathered on the back porch. Two men stood out, with weathered faces and familiar energy.

I struck up a conversation. They were first-timers, and firefighters. Frank, the more outgoing of the two, joked easily. His shoulders were relaxed like this was merely another adventure. Chad was different, with a heaviness about him.

Eventually, he shared that someone he loved had taken her own life. He carried the blame like a cross, convinced he should have been able to stop it.

He had tried everything—therapy, group counseling, self-medicating. Nothing helped. Ayahuasca was his last hope. He had fasted for three days before coming. That kind of dedication told me he was serious. Still, I saw the doubt in his eyes.

"What if it doesn't work?" he asked. "What if I can't connect?"

I told him about my first experience: the night I sat in silence while everyone else wept, purged, or saw visions. How it took another try before I finally cracked open.

"Surrender to it," I told him. "Let whatever comes up, come up. Don't hold it in. Cry. Scream. Laugh. Let it out." He exhaled, nodding slowly.

"Thank you," he replied. "I feel more at ease talking to you about it. I think I'm ready."

A splitting headache crept in. I excused myself and returned to my cabin to rest.

In the quiet of Cabin Nine, mine again by request, I let the headache settle into the pillow. Outside, I could hear distant voices—low, hopeful, and uncertain in the calm before the storm. I drifted into a light sleep, waiting for nightfall.

That evening, the group gathered in the temple. Only twelve this time, half first-timers, their faces a mix of anticipation and apprehension. Rosalia reminded us of the boundaries: no leaving for our cabins, no showers, no wandering outside the lighted pathways.

If we became overwhelmed, she encouraged us to step outside quietly rather than disrupt others. I wondered—had I been disruptive the night I processed Spencer's loss? Had my sobs intruded on someone else's journey?

I drank my medicine and settled in. "I am the student. I am here to learn whatever you see fit to teach me."

The medicine took its time, unfurling slowly, testing my patience. Over an hour passed before anything stirred within me. Finally, Her voice returned—a welcome sound in my mind.

"Take care of yourself. Stop running. Slow down."

I opened my eyes to see Frank at the altar. He was struggling to connect, searching for something that wouldn't come. His frustration was familiar. I sent him an unspoken prayer: *Let go. Trust it. Surrender.*

Chad, on the other hand, was deep in it. His cries echoed from outside the temple, raw and unrestrained. I didn't need to see him to know that he was breaking. The walls were crumbling. He was meeting his demons head-on. I hoped the ayahuasca would give him release and a path through the guilt to peace.

I tried not to focus on what Chad was going through, but I wondered if I was there that weekend to support him, as I'd felt others supporting me during my last retreat.

I had a small second cup, but was really content to just be.

Suddenly, Alex—the man immediately to my right—began beating on the ground, shouting, "I hate you! I hate you too!"

I sent him positive vibes. When that didn't work, I stepped outside and looked up at the sky. To my left, clouds flickered with lightning. One little star danced like a firefly. I tracked its path, and a vision appeared— an incredible, massive bust of a woman: a goddess.

"Mother Ayahuasca, is that you?" I whispered.

At that moment, lightning lit the sky, and she vanished, along with the cloud.

I laughed out loud. "Thank you for allowing me to see you."

A poem began to form in my mind—a message for my niece Danni, who was struggling to find her way. It was about the stars that shine behind the clouds, even when you cannot see them.

Of Spencer's three children, Danni was the one I had had the chance to grow closest to. Erin and I had assumed guardianship of her at the age of fifteen, jumping into parenting at the deep end and learning the hard way that teenage girls are more terrifying than war zones. Danni had had very little structure in her life before coming to live with us, and she needed it badly. The transition was anything but smooth.

She was also part of the reason I began researching the long-lasting impacts of childhood trauma. I needed to understand what I was seeing, so I could try to figure out how best to support her.

As my patience with the world around me dissolved, so did my patience with those at home. Danni turned eighteen in 2023, and I told her that she could no longer live under our roof if she refused to follow our rules. To be brutally honest, I kicked her out. It wasn't my best moment.

Thanks to Erin's grace and oversized heart, Danni landed softly at a college with a program in equestrian studies, her passion. Still, every conversation with Danni left me triggered and off-center. The gap in our parenting styles had also created serious tension between Erin and me.

Here with the medicine, a quiet realization settled in: Danni, so fiercely independent, was me. She had pushed me away, and I had let her. I had told myself it was her choice. Now, under the clearing sky, I saw the truth. Walking away had been my choice.

I vowed to reengage with her. Maybe, by offering guidance or simply being present for her, I could find a small measure of redemption for the times I had pushed away those who had tried to guide me.

My thoughts turned to Erin. Sometimes, life isn't about finding someone who shares your passions. It's about recognizing the person who shows up for you when it matters most.

I had gotten stuck thinking that a soulmate had to mirror me—my interests, my convictions, my search. Someone to talk about frequency and ancient civilizations over coffee. Someone on the same path. But what if a soulmate isn't your mirror? What if they're your anchor—a steady force that doesn't get swept up in your storm, but waits at the shoreline, holding space for your return?

Love isn't shared hobbies. It's shared protection. It's choosing each other, again and again—especially when things get hard.

I had been wanting Erin to seek what I was seeking, feel what I was feeling. Now I saw it differently. What could be more sacred than someone who protects you—even from yourself? Someone who doesn't need to walk your path or fully understand it, to support it? Someone who sees the parts of you you forget to honor—and holds them close until you're ready?

And then there was Amel.

Her love for Hazim had been so complete, so all-consuming, that she chose to walk into danger rather than imagine life without him. Not out of recklessness, but certainty. A love that didn't flinch in the face of death.

For so long, I'd carried the weight of her death, the guilt, the questions.

Finally, under that open sky, I felt her presence again, not as a wound, but as a cherished memory, and with an understanding that she was at peace and wanted me to be too.

"Thank you," I whispered, "for showing me what love really looks like. Not the kind that promises no sorrow, but the kind that refuses to let fear stand in the way."

An urgency stirred to put my thoughts to paper before they drifted away. As soon as the ceremony ended and I was back at my cabin, I opened my journal. The words flowed as if they'd been waiting for me to hear them. I called the poem, "Her Stars Above."

It was a prayer, really. Not that Danni would become something, but that she would remember that she already was.

CHAPTER 33

TRIAL BY SPIRIT

"Surrender is the simple but profound wisdom of yielding to rather than opposing the flow of life." –Eckhart Tolle

---

The next morning I asked Rosalia if she had any advice for the coming night. She smiled softly. "You have good guides. You do a good job of walking alone. Just surrender."

I hoped Mother Ayahuasca would be gentle with me, as She had been the previous night.

She wasn't.

As *La Medicina* took hold, a vision surfaced: a white porcelain claw-foot bathtub. I willed myself to climb inside. I already knew where this was going: Abandonment. Rejection. The wound that had never fully closed.

Warmth surrounded me. I felt safe, protected, and loved. A deep, instinctual knowing settled over me. I curled into a child's pose, forehead pressed against my pillow. I was passing through the birth canal. I felt pressure on all sides, then gasped for air.

I saw myself as a newborn, passed from one set of arms to another. First, my birth mother—nurturing, loving. Then, my adoptive father—his face full of hope, holding me like an answer to a prayer.

I had never doubted that I was loved, but for the first time, the weight of what that love had cost them both came into focus. They had given me a priceless opportunity, and I finally understood my need to prove that I had earned that sacrifice.

I thought about Mom and how difficult it must have been not to have the opportunity to have biological children. I recalled how awful I'd been to her as a teenager, and vowed to tell her I appreciated her.

A land mine appeared, massive and cartoonishly exaggerated, like something out of a Looney Tunes sketch. I whispered aloud, "What is that? Why is it there? What happens if it goes off?"

The voice answered, calm and steady. "You'll need more sacrament to follow that thread."

I hesitated. Did I really want to know?

I went to the altar with my cup. A short time later, the land mine detonated.

I was fourteen, lying on a dirty hotel room floor at the state championship track meet, with a boy from another school looming over me. I had not completely blocked the event from my memory, but I had never accepted it for what it was: sexual assault.

Thankfully, I found the courage to punch the kid in the face and extract myself from the situation before it went too far. Still, it went further than I wanted, and I felt dirty, used, and stupid.

That moment shaped my approach to deep connection and intimacy.

No one had done anything, because no one had known. Life went on. I put on my track uniform and kept running, just as I would put on my police uniform after the shooting and go back to work.

Rosalia was playing the sound bowls. I could feel the frequencies and see their waves flowing around and through me.

I was prompted to drink more sacrament, but my stomach revolted and my mind refused. I did not want any more, but I dug deep and willed myself to drink. I couldn't finish it and left the half-empty cup on the altar.

I did as you asked, I thought, settling in to see what was next.

Fables and stories from the Bible unfolded. Abraham had not needed to sacrifice his son; he had only needed to prove his willingness: a test of faith, not action.

The phrase "core principles" entered my mind. *What are my core principles? Integrity? Humility? Honor? Service? Must someone be tested on a principle in order to know if they live by it? Must we face trials to be found worthy?*

I had always been drawn to stories of epic quests; of heroes who defied the odds, rose to the occasion, and refused to bend a knee. I loved the ones who didn't set out to be heroes, but became ones through the trials they faced.

She told me to finish my cup. I felt nauseated. Was She testing me? I was desperate to be found worthy, and reluctantly went to the altar.

Rosalia seemed surprised. "You want more?" She asked.

"No," I cried. "But She is testing me."

"Go back to your mat. You are not ready," Rosalia lovingly told me.

I did as you asked. I went to the altar ready to drink.

Between the land mine from my youth and this feeling of being weighed and measured, I was spent.

154

CHAPTER 34
SOURCE CODE

"We don't heal in isolation, but in connection." –Unknown

As I entered the temple for the third night, Inti came to me and looked me in the eye. "Kemmi, Mother Ayahuasca will never test you."

I nodded, but his words sat heavy in the air. The night before had felt like a test, and one I barely passed. But his admonition was an echo of Rosalia's words earlier in the day, when I had suggested that Mother Ayahuasca had been hard on me: "You are the one who is hard on yourself."

I held onto their words as I turned my focus inward.

Some nights, She came as a whisper. Other nights, as a warning.

This night, She came as a hurricane.

The pain started in my abdomen—sharp, intense, and unrelenting. My first thought was that something was physically wrong with me. My appendix? My mind panicked, trying to assess the situation. This would be a terrible time to have a medical emergency.

Finally the realization hit: it was the sacrament.

Pain consumed me. Not just my body—my bones, my blood, my very being. There was no escape. No position eased it. I tried to make my way to the bathroom. I couldn't walk. I fell to my knees halfway down the walkway and sobbed. My body betrayed me in the most humbling way.

The words "I NEED HELP" appeared in my head like a neon sign.

With every ounce of my being, I did not want to say them.

The words clawed their way out of me. I hated saying them. I hated needing to. I also knew it was the whole point.

"I need help," I cried, through sobs so hard I wasn't sure I could be understood. I said it again, louder. "I need help, please."

One of the volunteers, Rosie, knelt beside me. "What do you need, dear?"

I couldn't stop crying. "I need help getting to the bathroom."

She took my arm, helped me to my feet, and supported me the rest of the way.

"Thank you for helping me," I managed between sobs.

She waited for me outside the bathroom and then helped me back to my mat.

My mind screamed at me. *Why do you keep doing this? Please make it stop.*

It didn't stop. It intensified. My body arched and twisted, writhing against whatever was being torn from me.

I needed to scream, and I didn't want to disturb the others. I had to get outside. I crawled on my hands and knees, dragging myself to the altar where Inti was sitting. My voice cracked as I whispered, "Please, can you help me outside?" Again, the act of requesting help was torture.

Inti lifted me to my feet and guided me out into the night air. I dropped to my hands and knees in the grass, and raw, guttural wails tore from my throat. Finally I purged, a release of something long overdue from deep inside of me.

The night stretched on. I didn't move. I lay in the grass, still wet from afternoon storms, as a swarm of mosquitoes surrounded me. Rosie tried to get me to go inside. "No. I need to feel the earth," I mumbled, so she covered me with a sheet.

I was overcome by an incredible thirst, but was still unable to move on my own. Another cry for help was answered, and my water bottle appeared beside me.

I felt cold and alone. "I need someone to be with me," I called out, barely above a whisper.

The pain began to subside. An angelic voice surrounded me. It was Rosalia, singing an Icaro, a medicine song, over me. The melody was like a thread pulling me back from the edges. It was a song about yielding— about letting the medicine move where it needed to go, and trusting what I could not see. Her voice wove healing through the layers of pain.

"Thank you," I murmured. "Thank you for being with me."

I was covered in grime, sweat, dirt, bugs, and bodily fluids. I spotted a hose nearby, the one we used to clean our little black buckets.

"Can someone help me?" I called out again. Rosie appeared.

"Can I rinse off with the hose?" I pleaded.

"Of course," she answered.

I kneeled as she ran water over my arms, my face, my legs. Then I lifted my head. "Can you run it over my head?"

Ice-cold, sulfur-scented water poured over me, washing away the night's battle. I gasped, then laughed.

Rosie joined in my laughter and wrapped a towel around my shoulders as she helped me inside.

As we approached the temple, something caught my attention—a small, fenced-off area in the dark. I felt drawn to it.

"Rosie," I whispered. "Can you remind me to ask Rosalia about that place?"

She pressed a hand to her heart and nodded.

Inti announced the last call for sacrament. I felt no pressure from Mother Ayahuasca. Yet, I knew that if I wanted to understand what I'd endured, I needed a little more.

I took my cup and went to the altar, smiling at Rosalia and pinching my thumb and forefinger together: "Only a tiny amount."

Rosalia returned the smile. "You are a warrior."

Tears welled up in my eyes as I whispered, "It's so hard." She nodded knowingly.

As I processed, I understood that corrupted source code had been ripped from every strand of DNA in my body. I watched as my neural pathways recalibrated. I had spent my life running outdated software, built on inherited fears and self-imposed limitations. Asking for help had felt impossible because I had built my identity on never needing it.

As a young woman, I had been determined not to be like my mother in her constant worry and need for control. Now, I wondered if that was her way of coping with her own fears. I realized, to my surprise, that I had adopted those traits after all.

I whispered a silent promise to myself. I would be a better daughter, a better spouse, a better friend. I would thank the people in my life for being in my life. I would tell them I loved them.

Rosalia asked if I was ready to close the ceremony. I joined the others, already gathered for the closing prayer. Afterward, I returned to my mat to finish processing the night. Hours passed before I joined the group on the porch. When I walked up the steps, the porch was abuzz with conversation. As I opened the door, it seemed that all eyes were on me.

Someone grinned. "What the hell happened to you?"

"My source code was rewritten."

Rosalia smiled, placing a hand over her heart. "Beautiful work."

Inti gleamed, "You survived!"

"Barely," I sighed.

Rosie reminded Rosalia about the small fenced-in area I had asked about.

Rosalia nodded. "That's a very special place. We only use it during the week-long winter retreat. During that time, there's a special ceremony in that space."

I dropped my head into my hands. "A week?! I'm gonna need some time to get behind that."

The whole porch erupted in laughter.

I had been stripped raw, torn apart, and put back together. And yet, I felt more whole than I had in my entire life.

I already knew I'd be coming for the winter retreat.

Dios Mio!

PART FIVE
THE LIVING VINE

CHAPTER 35

FEAR COMES KNOCKING

"It is not the fear of death that wears us down, but the fear of watching someone we love walk toward it." –Unknown

---

I had hoped to see Frank and Chad before they left, to see how they were doing after their experience. Sadly, they had decided not to stay for the third day.

I asked Inti to find out if they would be comfortable sharing their email addresses with me. A few days later, he sent me their contact information. I sent them each a message letting them know I was available if they ever wanted to talk or process what had happened.

Frank never responded. I hoped he wouldn't give up.

Chad told me he got what he needed the first two nights and had decided to leave early.

I had wanted to say so much more to him, to tell him how much I had felt his pain the first night and how I had prayed he would find peace. I was relieved to know he had found some healing, and wondered if he would feel the call to come back in time.

After the retreat, the changes I'd felt deepened.

Avoiding "low-frequency" activities—my new catch-phrase for anything that dragged me down—became easier. I had little desire to follow the news. The endless cycles of fear and outrage that had once consumed my attention were now noise—static designed to keep people anchored in place.

I wasn't afraid of what-ifs anymore. What if this happens? What if that happens? It didn't matter. The world was going to do what the world was going to do. I no longer felt the need to carry the weight of it on my shoulders.

The pull of old habits and old patterns didn't feel as strong. I felt freer, slept better, and was less anxious. The urge to eat junk food was lessened. My desire for alcohol faded even more. I spent more time outdoors. Maybe my code really had been rewritten.

I devoured the teachings of Eckhart Tolle, Don Miguel Ruiz, Joseph Campbell, Robin Wall Kimmerer, and others—not just reading, but absorbing. Each offered a different thread in the same tapestry: presence, transformation, myth, and reverence for the natural world. These weren't merely books. They were shifts in perspective, and reminders I wasn't alone—that countless others had walked this path before me.

I no longer carried resentment toward Danni, and felt able to begin again with her. I told Erin to let Danni take her cat to college, which had been a point of tension when she'd moved out, because I hadn't believed she was ready for that responsibility. But she had come to us with the cat. He was hers, and they needed each other. I was able to see that because I wasn't reacting from old wounds anymore.

I also found it easier to leave behind the identity of being a law enforcement officer. One day, I even stopped carrying my retirement credentials and gun. For the first time in decades, I didn't feel like I needed them to move safely through the world. I simply lost the need to be hyper-vigilant. I was no longer letting fear dictate my every step. It was liberating.

Within a week, I had committed to attending the winter retreat.

Then Erin was diagnosed with colon cancer.

———

When the diagnosis came, I didn't panic—at least not on the outside. I went into investigator mode: calm, logical, and focused. But beneath the calm was pure, unfiltered fear.

It wasn't just fear of losing Erin. It was fear of what the system might do to her. And underneath all of that was something deeper—something I hadn't been ready to confront.

I'd spent two decades protecting world leaders, guarding embassies, and managing crises. But when it really mattered, for the person I loved most, I was powerless. I couldn't stand between her and this. I couldn't intercept the threat.

And that truth—that I couldn't protect her—triggered something old and raw. My logical mind knew it wasn't failure, but it sure felt like failure—complete and unresolvable. Fear surfaced, even though I had sworn I had let fear go.

One minute she had stomach cramps, the next she was in the ER, and by the end of the week she'd been diagnosed with cancer of the sigmoid colon. She was scheduled for emergency surgery. There wasn't time to process it. No warning, no slow buildup. Just a freight train barreling through our lives.

I worried that if the doctors recommended chemo or radiation, she would say yes. She trusted them. She didn't question things the way I did. I worried that her treatment options might be influenced by factors beyond her actual medical needs.

Only a few months before, a friend in Florida had been diagnosed with breast cancer. All she wanted was to have the tumor removed. The doctors recommended chemo first, calling it the "standard of care," and hinted that her insurance might not cover surgery by itself. Other previous experiences had already eroded my trust in the medical system's ability to put patients before profits.

So, once again, I dove into research—medical journals, patient stories, anything that might offer a sense of control in the uncontrollable. The deeper I went, the more powerless I felt. I didn't know how I would handle it if Erin chose a path I didn't believe in. How could I say, "Please don't let them break you in the name of saving you. Please don't let the cure be worse than the disease"?

As I tried to stay grounded, I saw that my distrust of systems still held sway. The part of me that had found its safety in questioning everything—governments, institutions, protocols—wasn't fully healed.

Questioning rules and dogma had always been part of who I was. It had made me good at my job. But somewhere along the way, questioning hardened into fear—the kind that scans constantly for threats and begins to assume corruption as the default.

Throughout my career, I had prided myself on discernment and discretion. I hadn't noticed how that posture had bled into my personal life, where it turned into suspicion of everything. Integration allowed me to notice where my questioning was coming from, and to ask better questions, rooted in curiosity and a genuine desire to understand, rather than from reflexive distrust.

Thankfully, Erin's doctors were respectful. They listened. There was no pressure, no sales pitch, no scare tactics. When they told us no chemo or radiation was needed, only increased follow-ups and bloodwork, I finally exhaled.

She spent about a week in the hospital before beginning recovery at home. A melancholy fell over her as she recovered from surgery. Wanting to lift her mood, I suggested, "Let's go to Maui."

Since our wedding seven years prior, we had often talked about going back. We were planning to go for our ten-year anniversary. "Why wait?" I asked. We'd just been reminded how fragile life can be.

She loved the idea, and within an hour, we'd purchased plane tickets and reserved a VRBO in Kihei. I hoped Maui would help us reconnect and heal.

CHAPTER 36
MANIFESTING SEA TURTLES

"We are not human beings having a spiritual experience. We are spiritual beings having a human experience." –Pierre Teilhard de Chardin

On the flight to Maui, I began reading *The Magic* by Rhonda Bryne. I had read her book *The Secret*, and believed there was truth in the idea that our thoughts shape our reality. The book outlined daily gratitude practices designed to take manifestation to the next level and emphasized starting each day from a place of gratitude, so I decided to try it.

Each morning, I sat with my coffee and scribbled ten things I was grateful for, followed by wishes for the coming day, into the pages of my notebook—anything from parking spaces and sunrises to feelings of peace and love.

One morning, I jotted down my desire for "a smooth drive to Wai'ānapanapa along the famous Road to Hana, and a breathtaking sunrise."

We got the necessary early start and encountered virtually no traffic. We pulled off at a roadside stop to use the restroom. As I was walking to the car, I saw the sun break the horizon over the ocean. We walked over to the railing and watched a sunrise so stunning it moved me to tears. The rest stop was elevated above the canopy of trees that lined the road, giving us a clear view of the ocean. Had we stayed on the road a few more minutes, we would have missed the sunrise.

It kept happening—small wishes turning into reality, as if the Universe was listening.

The next morning, I wrote: "I am grateful for the smooth drive up Mount Haleakalā to see the sunrise. For the primo parking spot. For the amazing clear sky and low winds. For a sunrise with all the colors of the rainbow."

As I wrote it, I hesitated. *Why did I write "all the colors of the rainbow"? That makes no sense.*

Our first trip to Haleakalā years before had been brutal—freezing winds and thick cloud cover that swallowed the sunrise whole. This time, the road was empty. We reached the summit and got the very last parking space at the small upper-summit lot.

As the sun began to rise, I turned my gaze west, and there it was: the entire sky behind me, painted in perfect gradients. Every color of the rainbow stretched across the sky, from violet in the west to red in the east.

Another day we decided to go to Iao Valley. As we approached, a sign read, "Reservations Required to Enter Iao Valley." We pulled off the road to see if we could make a reservation. It was 7:29 am. We made a reservation for 7:30 am.

That morning, I had manifested, "The trail to the private swimming hole unfolded before us as if it were lighted." Again, I questioned myself—*What am I writing?*

As we walked along the valley floor by the river, I noticed a narrower pathway that followed the bank uphill. It was shaded, with trees growing along both sides, but the sun was just high enough that light came through the canopy of the trees and lighted the trail.

We followed it and found the most exquisite little pool. I eased myself in and swam slowly through the ice-cold water. It was so quiet even the birds seemed to whisper. There was a large, smooth rock jutting out of the center of the pool. I climbed up on it and sat there in the stillness for several minutes of sheer gratitude and enjoyment.

I hoped Erin might join me. Instead, she slipped off her shoes and socks and sat on the bank, taking in the beauty of the place in her own way. She shook her head in amusement at my tendency to immerse myself in freezing waterfalls, mountain streams, and lakes.

While we were sitting on the beach one night watching the sun set, the lyrics to a song popped into my head: the Mormon primary school song "I Am a Child of God," which I'd not heard or thought of since childhood.

The chorus goes:

Lead me, guide me,

Walk beside me,

Help me find the way.

Teach me all that I must do

To live with Him someday.

I was perplexed and actually a little annoyed that these words had come to me, but they would not leave my head.

The next day, we stopped by a roadside vendor selling carved whale tails, Hawaiian gods, and sea turtles. We had wanted a carved whale's tail since our first visit. As we negotiated on a small one, Erin noticed a sea turtle with a striking appearance. The wood was deep black, different from the other pieces. Curious, she asked about it. The artist told her the wood had come from Lahaina.

I got chills. We loved Lahaina on our first visit. We had driven through the area on this visit and could still see the devastation from the 2023 fire.

As we drove off with our whale tale, I thought about the turtle, about alchemy, and about transformation born from devastation. A scar could be turned into something meaningful, almost sacred.

After lunch that day, we decided to go for a walk on the beach. Erin was hoping to see some sea turtles, so I made an attempt at an on-the-move manifestation.

As we walked onto the beach, we noticed several people standing around something that looked like a big rock. As we got closer, we realized it was a sea turtle, having a rest on the sand. We sat nearby, far enough not to disturb it, enjoying the company of something so majestic.

A woman walked by and told us there was a group of turtles that had been sleeping on that very beach at night for the past few weeks. We returned after sunset, and sure enough, they were there, nestled on the sand in the glow of a full moon—just in case we needed a little more blessing on the moment.

We kept our distance and took a few photos, careful not to let the flash go off and disturb the turtles. Then we crouched in the sand, hushed and reverent, blinking slowly in time with the turtles. A smile spread across Erin's face, with no trace of worry, illness, or statistics. Just moonlight. Her hand slipped into mine, and neither of us spoke. We didn't need to.

We returned to the roadside vendor the following day and claimed the Lahaina-wood sea turtle as our own. We named her Kiah—a Hawaiian name, meaning "rise and breathe." It was a prayer, both for Erin and for the two of us together.

CHAPTER 37
MOSES

"Worry does not empty tomorrow of its sorrow, it empties today of its strength." –Corrie Ten Boom

---

The more I leaned into the flow of life, the more undeniable it became. Synchronicity had become my everyday reality. At first it was amusing, then natural. I stopped second-guessing it and simply trusted. The less I worried, the less I needed to.

Spirituality was no longer something I felt externally. It was something I was living internally. Each morning, before anything else, I began my day with a prayer. Not out of obligation or because I thought I was supposed to, but because I wanted to. I spoke directly, expressing gratitude, setting my intentions, asking for guidance, and trusting that what was meant for me would unfold in its own time.

Meanwhile, I grew impatient with those I loved who were still tethered to cycles of worry—my brother Rees, my mother, even Erin at times. I knew they were doing the best they could, but it was hard to sit in conversations that revolved around worst-case scenarios, fear, and things no one could control.

Once I saw how the world responds to the energy we put out, it became harder to tolerate the weight of constant negativity. I redoubled my efforts to focus on my growth and studies. I found solace in an unused loft space in the house and turned it into my sanctuary. I filled it with books, small tokens from meaningful events in my life, and a few of Dad's things. I even added an altar with gemstones and a candle where I could sit quietly, meditate, and pray.

I invited teachings from all religions into my studies. The core messages —love, faith, trust—were the same, regardless of the path that delivered them. In the last set of ceremonies, Mother Ayahuasca had been clear that it's the message that matters, not the doctrine.

One day, taking a break from working on the building, I turned on the TV. I flipped through options with no actual intention and landed on a Netflix series about Moses. I didn't plan to watch the whole thing, but I did. The fact that I binge-watched anything surprised me. That I binge-watched something religious had me shaking my head with a laugh.

I was struck by several elements of Moses' story. I was not interested in comparing myself to a Biblical prophet, but there were parallels I couldn't ignore: he was adopted, he was outraged by the mistreatment of others, and he had walked away from the world he knew, leaving behind his title to follow a call.

Not long after watching the series, Erin and I spent a brutally cold weekend in Kansas City. In a charming bookstore called Prospero's, I stumbled upon a used copy of *Moses: In the Footsteps of the Reluctant Prophet* by Adam Hamilton. Earlier that same day, over lunch with two high school friends I hadn't seen in years, one mentioned a classmate we used to call "Mose."

It was insignificant in any logical sense, but it was another nudge: first a show, next a bookstore, and finally a friend called "Mose." It wasn't coincidence—it was a breadcrumb trail I was being asked to follow.

When I was prompted to climb the mountain behind the house, I seriously wondered if I was losing it.

Yet for months, I had been meaning to make time to climb to the bluff. It had been years since I'd been to the top, but I thought about it often. I made a mental note to climb it before I left for the winter retreat. I didn't know what I'd find there, only that I felt a quiet but insistent call to go.

The building was coming along slowly but steadily. Each step forward reflected my own journey: plans shifted as the vision became more clear, and more than once, I made changes on the fly, as walls were going up.

The winter retreat was on the horizon. I had no expectations, only a deep knowing that I was meant to go.

A few days before I left for Florida, I took advantage of an unseasonably warm day to keep my promise to myself to climb the mountain. I texted my neighbor for permission to cross her land and to warn her I might show up shirtless on any game cameras, soaking up vitamin D.

I grabbed a water bottle, laced up my hiking shoes, and set off. The trail was familiar—or so I thought.

At the top, I soaked up the view and prayed for guidance on my retreat. I also asked to understand why I was there. I wondered how many others across time had stood on that bluff and talked to God.

Shortly after purchasing the Middle Ground, I'd met an older man whose family had lived on the property when he was a boy. He wanted permission to walk the land, and I freely gave it.

One day, we walked the land together. He showed me things I would not have found on my own. He asked if he could dig out the spring, long buried under layers of silt and time, that his family had used for drinking water and to keep the goat milk cool in the summer months. A few months later, I returned to find cold, crystal-clear water flowing up from the earth from a small concrete opening that had been carefully excavated.

He also pointed out a pear tree, half-hidden in the tangle of kudzu. The vines had nearly choked it out. He told me that the tree was over fifty years old and had once been part of an orchard. I cleared the vines away, letting the old tree breathe. It came alive, producing more fruit that year than we could use. We made jelly and shared it with friends and family. It still stands today, choosing in its old age when to bloom and when to rest.

We hiked up the mountain together on one of those crisp Ozark days when the blue sky stretches wide over the valley below. As we rested on the rocks, he began to talk about God. I bristled. Who was he to talk to me about God? He didn't know me, didn't know what I believed or did not believe.

After that, I kept my distance, ending the relationship poorly. I wondered if it were too late to change that. As a boy, had he climbed to the bluff and talked to God? Just as the Osage may have done before us?

On the way down the mountain, I got completely turned around. I laughed and muttered, "Well, that's poetic. I'm literally lost in the wilderness."

I had always been terrible at reading maps. In twenty years as a DS agent, my biggest fear wasn't gunfire, it was being asked to plan motorcade or evacuation routes. Fortunately—for all parties involved—that never happened.

I pulled out my phone, trying to orient myself. Nothing made sense. The woods didn't look familiar. The view of the valley below didn't look familiar. I had no idea which direction would take me to the house.

I called Erin. "If I go downhill, I have to hit the trail that leads home, right?"

"Yeah, if you're on the right side of the mountain."

I laughed at first. Of course I was on the right side. But as I scanned the unfamiliar terrain, realization crept in: I wasn't. I had completely missed something obvious.

I hadn't climbed the mountain to sit at the top, but to get lost. To be reminded that even on the spiritual path, we can miss things that should be obvious. We must keep asking, listening, seeking, learning, and growing.

Like Moses wandering the desert, I needed to lose the trail for a while.

There was a brief moment when fear crept in like it used to. That old, familiar anxiety rose within me, whispering stories of uncertainty and doubt. The old version of me would have spiraled, trying to control and overthink. This time, I stayed calm. I breathed. And I chose to trust the unfolding.

I found my way home. Sadly, a quick search revealed that my old exploring buddy had passed only a few weeks earlier.

CHAPTER 38
I REMEMBER

I left the building in the capable hands of my buddy, who was likely relieved not to have to provide oversight to me for a few weeks.

It was not easy to pull myself away. The drywall was nearly finished, the ceilings prepped, the details taking shape; it was an exciting time to be there. I was watching a dream slowly become real.

I made the long drive from the Ozarks to South Florida, determined not to let myself get sucked into the noise of the world along the way. Instead, I pressed play on *The Alchemist*—a book I'd read long ago and had been wanting to revisit. As the miles stretched before me, I was struck by the poetry of Santiago's journey: how everything had come full circle, and every detour, every so-called mistake, had been necessary to bring him exactly where he was meant to be. Every setback was part of his greater path.

On the way, I stopped to spend an afternoon with Danni at her school in central Florida. Since my first two retreats, there was an ease between us now that hadn't been there before: less guardedness, more space just to be together.

We talked about old wounds—really talked. For the first time, I was able to see those early years through the eyes of a scared fifteen-year-old who had already lost both parents, one to homicide and one to drugs. She came to us carrying more trauma than any child should have to bear, along with coping patterns that made sense given what she'd survived.

It had been clear that she needed structure. What hadn't been clear to me at the time was how my own fear shaped the way I delivered that structure.

I told her how scared we had been for her future—how the rules, the intensity, and the course-correcting came from a deep desire to protect her from what we perceived as danger zones. And as I listened to her, I could see how my reactions had also been shaped by my own history— by a childhood where anger surfaced faster than comfort, and control often stood in for safety.

She told me I was mean. She wasn't wrong.

I told her I was sorry.

We talked for hours, in the kind of conversation that leaves you lighter, as if something heavy has finally been set down. When we parted ways, any tension, resentment, or unspoken hurt between us was gone.

I headed south, back to the temple. When I stepped onto the porch, I was shocked to see Alex. What were the odds he would come back at the same time? And not only Alex, but also Camila, originally from Brazil, who had been beside Alex at our last retreat.

I remembered Camila fondly because she'd spent much of my source code ceremony laughing. What a trio: I'd been outside the temple screaming at the top of my lungs as corrupted code was ripped from my body, Alex was inside yelling at himself and purging disgusting images from his psyche, and Camila had been laughing gleefully.

We had a joyful reunion. Alex and I had unknowingly already set up our spaces next to one another. We invited Camila to join us, and I wondered if we were meant to be there together again.

While there were only eleven participants (two men and nine women), it was a diverse group. There were people from overseas living in the United States, an artist from Tajikistan, single people, married people, some with kids, others with no kids. There was a woman around my age, maybe slightly older, who struggled to turn in her phone. She had a great deal of anxiety over not being able to talk to her adult children, even though she'd given them Inti's contact info.

The week would include five ayahuasca ceremonies, a crystal ceremony, and the Rite of Inner Resurrection ceremony, held in the garden that had called to me. We would take a vow of silence as we'd done in the three-day retreats, and eat a vegetarian diet.

I had struggled with hunger during my first retreat, but by the second, it had eased. My cravings for food had dissipated since I'd started this journey. I'd lost nearly twenty pounds without trying. I also noticed less of a desire to eat red meat or pork, even outside of the thirty-day windows when I followed *la Dieta*.

My intention for the first ceremony was simple: *Remember who you are.*

Recently I had read *Be Here Now* by Ram Dass. Erin had given it to me the year before as a slightly ironic birthday gift, because it had been one of the most popular books in the year I was born.

The theme "remember who you are" runs through the book and wouldn't let me go. I kept thinking: *What does it mean, "remember who you are"?*

One night before bed, a week or so after I devoured the book, I whispered a quiet request to the Divine: "Help me understand. Help me remember who I am."

The next morning, I woke up with a phrase flashing in my mind's eye like a neon sign: Be Still.

The words drew me to the stillness of infancy—the kind of stillness that comes not from immobility, but from the inability to express ourselves in words. The kind of awareness that exists before judgment, before questioning, before understanding—when we simply watch the world from car seats, strollers, and our parents' arms, taking it all in. Childhood memories came flooding in—playing alone in my room with Star Wars figurines or model horses.

My parents had told me about panicking when they couldn't find me, only to discover I'd gotten tired and put myself to bed—which was something I still did. Some people call that an "Irish goodbye." Erin's family calls it "pulling a Kemmi."

As a teen, I'd go jogging around the lake development where we lived. I ran for miles, usually when I was upset, which was often. I'd end up at the top of the hill with the water tower, the cool wind in my face, able to see for miles around me.

In the crawl space above my bedroom was a box of old journals and papers going all the way back to junior high school. I sifted through the box until I found the essay, "Contemplation in Solitude," that I'd written more than thirty years prior.

It spoke of a young, angry girl who had stormed off, wanting to be left alone, and had found comfort in nature. The last line read: "It's amazing how something so beautiful and simple as nature can make things seem just that—simple."

Perhaps "remember who you are" was reminding me to be true to the core aspects of my personality: the parts of me that had always been drawn to nature, to writing, to solitude. To be still, and listen to myself.

As my mind began to follow the medicine, I was surprised to feel a male presence this time, which was guiding me to a series of stories from my childhood.

From the time I was old enough to bend down and pick things up, I would fill my pockets with rocks. I once refused to leave a store until my parents bought a geode from the display case. I still had it. Once, Erin and I hiked up a mountain in Guatemala and I hiked down with a backpack full of stone treasures.

I was an animal lover and rescuer, starting with a feral kitten I found and brought home. He became my constant companion, even finding his way home after a vet visit gone wrong.

I had a healthy dose of righteous indignation. According to Mom, one of the popular girls in kindergarten told me I couldn't be in her club if I was friends with Alissa. Mom said my response was, "I don't care about being in your club, I like Alissa."

All of these memories filled my heart with a deep knowing that I had always been a good person.

Before becoming a law enforcement officer, I had considered becoming a counselor or therapist. I recalled Santiago's journey in *The Alchemist* and chuckled out loud. If I had gone into that line of work right out of college, I would never have gained the life experience and understanding of human suffering I'd earned through my career and travels around the world.

I asked my new guide to help me understand why I had chosen to become a cop when I hated rules. Especially arbitrary, outdated, tyrannical, or otherwise capricious rules: laws and regulations that did not pass the common-sense sniff test.

Simple answer: officer discretion. The ability to right wrongs, and to use common sense to apply the intent of the law rather than the letter of the law. I took great pride in applying this principle throughout my career, often opting for lectures and warnings over tickets and arrests.

A sense of peace came over me: peace with who I was, and a reassurance that I was on the right path.

My new guide was not as demanding. The ceremony was free of the chaos and physical pain I'd come to expect. I felt only mild discomfort —the kind that forces you to sit with yourself. I asked Rosalia for a small second cup.

She placed her hand over her heart. "Remember who you are."

My jaw dropped. "Did you really just say that?"

She smiled and repeated, "Remember who you are."

Back at my mat, there came a whisper: "You've always been a healer— you just wore a badge, and carried a gun instead of a notepad." My new guide didn't speak as much as nudge: *Slow down. Be still. Trust the unfolding.*

My thoughts drifted to my birth mother. We'd only met twice, and exchanged a few emails over the years. It wasn't a relationship so much as a sense of past connection. I'd always let her lead the pace of contact, unsure how much she wanted.

I wondered if my new guide could be Dad. Maybe the memories that surfaced of my childhood were his.

When I shared the experience with Rosalia the next day, she listened intently, and said gently, "You are ready."

"For what?"

"To heal your relationships with both your mothers. Your birth mother, and the mother who raised you. Not only did she do the best she could, she did a beautiful job."

Her words landed with surprising ease. I wasn't defensive or guarded. I simply nodded.

She smiled. "You've come a long way from the woman I first met. Back then, you were—intimidating."

I laughed. "I get that a lot."

She was right; I had softened. I had laid down the armor—because I no longer needed it. Healing hadn't been about shedding pain. It had been about remembering the gentleness underneath it all: the me I'd buried beneath a blanket of Kevlar.

CHAPTER 39

THE ONES WHO SHAPED ME

"We write to taste life twice, in the moment and in retrospect." –
Anaïs Nin

I walked mostly alone the next night. My new guide was present only briefly at the beginning and again at the close. He told me to embrace my inner child, to imagine being an infant: to see myself crying to have my needs met, and to see my mother coming to comfort and care for me.

Rosalia was right. Despite our sometimes tense relationship, my mother had done her best.

I had adopted traits from both of my adoptive parents. And, if I liked who I was (which I did), then why would I wish to change anything about the past? The thought came, *You have always been exactly where you needed to be at the exact moment you needed to be there.*

From Dad, I learned love, laughter, compassion, service, work ethic, and empathy. He had a great sense of humor and a laugh you could hear across a crowded room. As a teenager it made me cringe, but it became one of the things about him I missed the most.

Dad was rarely angry. Calm by nature, he had the look of a dentist, if there is such a thing: trustworthy, approachable, and smart. His manner was friendly and engaging, though I suspect he would have been labeled an introvert on any credible personality test.

He loved tinkering and building things, and had once dreamed of becoming an engineer. I wish I'd written the story down when he told me how he ended up as a dentist instead. Anytime I had a science project, he was all in. I made a volcano and several other projects from the materials used to make dentures and take impressions.

He taught me to drive a manual by letting me shift gears from the passenger seat, training my ear to the sound of the engine.

He had a sweet tooth despite his profession. On days I worked in his office after school, we'd sometimes stop at the Tastee Freeze before heading home. "Don't tell your mother," he'd say, passing me a frozen treat.

He was my biggest fan and supporter. When I dreamed of becoming an Olympic athlete and insisted on training after track practice at night, he followed behind in the car, headlights illuminating the road ahead. He believed in me so fiercely that I had no choice but to believe in myself. He led me to find my calling as a law enforcement officer, and I always tried to make him proud.

My biggest regret was that I never got to say goodbye. I returned from El Salvador and landed in St. Louis late the night before his emergency surgery. By the time I saw him, he was in a coma. If only I'd arrived earlier, or gone by the hospital after visiting hours, or gone early before they took him to surgery. I didn't understand how serious it was until it was too late.

As much as I had modeled myself after my father, my mother had also given me exactly what I needed in order to become who I was meant to be.

Where she worried, I became fearless. Where she exhibited anxiety, I developed an insatiable desire to understand the human mind, including my own. Even after earning a minor in psychology, that hunger never faded. It became a tool that served me well in interviews with both victims and suspects.

Her desire to be needed made me fiercely independent and taught me how to armor up. Her sometimes difficult countenance helped me to develop patience and diplomacy—skills that became invaluable in my life and career. Her fear of failure and doubts in my abilities gave me an unstoppable "yes I can" attitude and a desire to succeed no matter what.

Those traits, I now understood, shaped me as much as Dad's belief in me ever had.

As a high school freshman, I broke the school record in the 1600-meter run. On the final lap, I gave it everything I had, pushing my body to its absolute limit, and my bladder staged a small rebellion and let loose. It was a moment of sheer exhaustion, exhilaration, and humiliation.

Dad wasn't there that day, but Mom was. I raced to the stands, breathless and proud. "I broke the record!" I told her.

Her reply? "Are you sure their clocks weren't broken?"

I was crushed.

Now, I saw it differently. She wasn't trying to hurt me. She was trying, in her own way, to protect me from the sting of disappointment.

It was ironic, really, because her caution became the fuel that drove me, the reason I refused to quit, and the reason I kept showing up, even when it sucked.

More than once, there were moments during retreats when I thought about getting in my truck and driving home. I knew I wouldn't quit, though, and I had Mom to thank for that.

A melody came into my head. It was that damn Mormon primary song again. I began to hum it softly, then to sing the lyrics ever so quietly, through soft tears. It wasn't just the chorus I had recited on the beach in Maui, but the whole first verse:

I am a child of God,

And He has sent me here.

Has given me an earthly home

With parents kind and dear.

Lead me, guide me,

Walk beside me,

Help me find the way.

Teach me all that I must do

To live with Him someday.

I wanted to sing it properly, which felt comical. The last time I had sung it was in front of the entire congregation, around age eleven. From a front pew, a friend had laughed at me. It was the last time I'd ever done a solo act.

I stepped outside to my spot by the fire pit, under the clear sky. I faced the moon and sang the song three times, a little louder each time, voice cracking, tears still streaming down my cheeks. The moon stood witness, steady and full, as if it had been waiting for me to find my voice.

Years ago, I had sung to the moon, hoping that somewhere out there, someone was listening. There were so many nights growing up when I looked up at the moon and whispered questions I didn't know how to ask anyone else. Was I wanted? Was I seen? Was I alone?

The moon never answered—not in words—but she never left, either.

She kept watch over me. Even when I was away from home and didn't feel at home where I was, she followed me from city to city, country to country, mission to mission. She was a quiet witness, a distant mother, a reminder that somewhere beyond logic and lineage, I belonged.

I used to imagine her as the one thing that connected me to my birth mother: some celestial cord that stretched between us.

The moon was a reflection of all the parts I wasn't ready to face, all the questions I'd buried.

She was also a reflection of all the light I still carried, despite the shadows. The moon doesn't shine with her own light; she reflects it. And maybe that's what we're all doing, those of us who choose to heal: reflecting the light that's always been there, letting it reach someone else, in case they're standing in the dark.

CHAPTER 40

THE LITTLE GARDEN

"The fire that warms us can also consume us; it is not the fault of
the fire." –Swami Vivekananda

On the third day of the retreat, we took a break from ayahuasca for the
ceremony I had anticipated most.

Rosalia explained its purpose: to heal maternal wounds and reconnect
with Mother Earth. When her guides first gave it to her, she thought it
was crazy, burying people up to their necks in sand. However, her
research revealed ancient roots for the practice, which symbolized
death of the ego and being reborn in the spirit—a way of remembering
that the Earth is both cradle and teacher.

We gathered in the early afternoon. Rosalia assigned each of us a spot
in the garden, marking lines in the sand so we'd know where to dig.
The sand was soft, the digging easy.

I laid down and let Rosalia and the staff cover me with cool sand. Its
weight was like an embrace from the Earth, protective and nurturing.

I focused on letting go of the heaviness I'd been carrying and releasing it into the ground. A restless energy pulsed in my lower abdomen—my root chakra, the seat of stability and security. I wasn't sure why it always gathered there, but it did.

I tensed and released my muscles, guiding the stuck energy through my feet and head, until it dissolved into the Earth. Afterward, I showered and returned to my cabin. The constant chatter in my mind had quieted. I slept deeply and peacefully.

The next morning, I told Rosalia that I had felt something release. She told me that as I'd dug, I'd gone off course from the line she'd drawn for me. She laughed softly. "It's fitting," she said. "Almost symbolic— you didn't choose the space I assigned. You picked a different mother." Then, more gently, "There's meaning in everything that happens. Even the things we don't realize we're choosing."

"Any guidance for tonight?" I asked.

"Just stay open."

Through the day, the quiet of the sand still clung to me—a calm I carried into the ceremony. I said a silent prayer to Mother Ayahuasca, asking her to connect me to the ancestors and show me how I fit into this great web of life.

The ceremony which followed was unlike any before or since. It shattered every expectation, plunging me into a world of color, prophecy, and ancestral wisdom.

For the first time, I experienced what many people assume all psychedelic journeys to be: visions awash in brilliant colors, a feeling of being transported to another time and place. Until now, my journeys had been mostly internal, like a guided dialogue with subtle visuals, muted tones, and gentle impressions.

But on this night, before I could begin my usual gentle rocking, a vivid vision exploded in my mind's eye. A gorgeous roll of fabric unfurled before me. It was white, with delicate yellow and green squares woven into the cloth, handmade by Indigenous women. It rolled out like a pathway, leading me forward, as if I had been invited to a sacred gathering that had existed long before I arrived.

A vast arena stretched before me—built not of stone and mortar, but of the earth itself. The walls were a deep, sunbaked adobe, curved and smooth like something shaped by ancient hands over centuries. The floor was packed clay, worn soft from generations of footsteps. In the center, a bonfire burned, its flames reaching toward the sky.

Generations of women sat in long rows, draped in woven fabrics adorned with intricate patterns of red, yellow, and orange dots. Mothers, daughters, and granddaughters, an unbroken lineage of feminine power stretching into the past and the future. Their backs were to me, their focus forward, waiting. Their painted garments gleamed under the firelight.

Above the arena, a chief floated in the sky. His large, feathered headdress flowed around him. Beside him, several silhouetted figures hovered in the darkness. I couldn't see their faces, but I knew—they were the ancestors.

I longed to speak with them and began rising out of my body, floating up toward their presence.

Then Alex suddenly erupted beside me. A torrent of negative energy and verbal outbursts shattered the moment. The ancestors scattered like smoke in the wind.

"No, no, no, please come back," I begged. But they were gone.

Frustration surged through me, an almost physical ache. They had left before I could understand why they'd come. I didn't know if they'd ever come back.

I grabbed my blanket and water bottle and stepped outside, needing air, needing space, and needing them to come back to me.

I grabbed a yoga mat from the lounge room and reclaimed my spot by the fire pit. I laid down, covered myself with my blanket, closed my eyes, and begged them to come back and speak with me. I asked them to teach me about religion as they had known it.

I felt their presence return, quiet but unmistakable.

They told me that their church was never made of stone. Their church was nature itself. They said we had forgotten our duty to be stewards of the land and had severed our connection to the sacred.

They told me they were proud of me and that I should continue to seek out direct communication with the Divine.

I looked at the sky above me and saw two massive cloud formations. On the right was the profile of an ancient man with a full beard: Moses. The prophet who had walked between worlds, who had led his people through the wilderness, who had spoken to the Divine without a middleman.

On the left was a raven. Its form was not flesh and feather, but carved, like the totems of the Indigenous: a sacred messenger.

Both figures bore a single, luminous star as their eye—piercing, watchful, knowing. Neither cloud formation changed in the slightest. The images were frozen. I continued to look at them, trying to deduce their meanings.

I asked if there was anything else I needed to know, and the Chief said I had everything I needed. I thanked him for teaching me.

I thought of the generations of women from the vision—so many strong, grounded women who had come before. I hadn't always known how to connect with that kind of strength. I could feel the feminine energy stirring in me—not as something to resist, but as something to embrace.

It wasn't about being soft or hard, strong or weak. It was about being whole. It had taken me nearly five decades to accept that.

There was grief in that. Grief for all the years I had worn armor when I longed to be held. Grief for the ways I'd numbed myself in the name of strength.

But there was also gratitude. I had made it here, back to myself. In surrender, I sensed her returning: the woman inside me who didn't need to grip the reins so tightly, but who could still stand with quiet confidence and not care what others thought.

Alex was outside yelling angrily, "God, where are you? Where are you, God?"

I whispered quietly to myself, "Everywhere."

CHAPTER 41
MESSAGE RECEIVED

"If you're going through hell, keep going." –Winston Churchill

---

Ok, what else do I need to see?

My mind lit up with a flicker of electricity. I braced myself. *Oh boy*, I thought. *What now?*

It was a memory from high school. A memory of perhaps the only time I knew my dad had really been disappointed in me. I worked at Dad's office after school, which meant I had keys. And—I may have used the dental office as a make-out spot once or twice.

As luck would have it, one of those times was a night Dad had to come back to the office for something.

Imagine his surprise when he came into the lobby and found a couple of kids making out. I was in the darkroom with my boyfriend, and there was another couple in one of the operatories.

The memory hit with the force of a sucker punch. The shame was still there, tucked away, waiting to be acknowledged. I had been caught doing something I didn't want Dad to know about. I had let down the one person whose respect meant everything. I had violated his trust, and I saw it in his face—the heavy, quiet disappointment that doesn't need words.

I said to my guide, "Now you're just trying to embarrass me."

He answered with quiet certainty: "This is part of your story. The authentic story. Embarrassment, shame, guilt—these emotions linger in the dark, turning toxic when ignored. You must face them. If left buried, they poison the body and break relationships."

Ugh. Fine.

I had a nagging thought that my house was burning down. It wasn't completely irrational. The property was wooded and remote, and there had recently been controlled burns nearby.

Even after the ceremony ended, I couldn't shake it. The front door of the staff house was open, and through the storm door I saw Inti standing in the kitchen. I tapped gently on the glass. He stepped outside, calm as always. "Yes, my dear. What do you need?"

"Inti," I said, "I can't shake the feeling my house is burning down. Can I text my brother to check on things?"

He smiled. "Your house is fine. Your body is your house. If the sacrament says your house is on fire, it's you. You should speak with my mother about this tomorrow."

I nodded, feeling only slightly reassured.

The next morning, as I cleaned my space in the temple, I noticed that the space of the woman who had found it difficult to be without her phone was empty.

I wondered if, like Chad, the New York firefighter, she believed she had gotten what she needed. Or was being unplugged from the outside world too much? Or did the sacrament show her more than she was ready to see?

Later, I told Rosalia about the fire.

"So," she said gently, "you have work still to do."

I wasn't sure I liked that insight.

Apprehension crept in. But I recalled something my new guide had told me on the first night: "Learn to be comfortable in the discomfort." I exhaled.

That afternoon, I asked Rosie: "Do the ceremonies get easier?"

She paused before responding, "For me, it took three years before I could process quietly, without discomfort. It was the hardest thing I've ever done in my life—and also the most rewarding."

I nodded. I understood. Even on the nights when I whispered to myself, "For the love of God, never do this again," I wouldn't have traded it for anything.

Rosalia once told me that ayahuasca was like childbirth. "Women don't spend their lives thinking about how painful the delivery was. They wouldn't trade the suffering, because the end result was worth the pain."

I sat with that thought for a long time. Maybe my house was burning —but not down. Maybe the fire was part of the transformation.

I had a feeling the next ceremony would ask more of me.

As Mother Ayahuasca started her work that evening, I sensed a reckoning coming, something deep and painful. I took my blanket, water bottle, and bucket and headed outside. One of the staff had already set up a yoga mat and pillow for me in my spot.

I began screaming as my stomach ripped open. From inside, light poured out—an intense, golden light that was being pulled upward, drawn toward a greater, all-encompassing light in the sky.

The stuck energy I had carried for so long, the heaviness—it was them. The two pregnancies I had not carried to term. I had forgiven myself, but I had not asked them for forgiveness. I had not taken responsibility for my actions.

I had fractured my soul, leaving a wound that had never healed, and they had been waiting for me to recognize it.

For the first time during this retreat, I heard Her: Mother Ayahuasca, loud and unmistakable. "IT IS WRONG TO TAKE LIFE. PROTECT LIFE."

Again and again, the words came. The message was being hammered into me.

"YOU MUST UNDERSTAND. IT IS WRONG TO TAKE LIFE."

I sobbed. "I'm sorry. I'm so sorry."

I thanked them for choosing me. I apologized that I had not risen to the challenge, had not been the mother they deserved.

The pain eased, and Her voice softened slightly. "Everything that grows is alive. It's simple. When something requires endless justifications, you are bending it to fit your desires."

My irrational fear of suffocation emerged. As a volunteer firefighter in college, I had once walked through fire. It was both exhilarating and terrifying. Thick black smoke filled the room, and fire danced up the walls. Then the alarm on my oxygen tank went off. My air was running out. For a moment I couldn't even think.

I dropped to the floor, feeling my way backward along the fire hose to safety. The fear of suffocation never left me. It was the reason I had not continued down the path of becoming a firefighter.

La Medicina showed me the deeper connection: I had felt suffocated as a child, not physically, but energetically. Mom's world had been one of worry and fear. Her love, meant to protect, sometimes smothered me. A deep sadness washed over me. I had spent so much time resenting that energy, pushing against it, trying to break free.

Then the next connection formed: my mother had not been born afraid. She had become afraid, shaped by her own childhood, by pressures I had never considered. What did I really know about her childhood?

I knew she loved to go fishing with her father when she was a girl. I wanted to recreate that memory for her, and made a plan to schedule a fishing trip for her and Rees, to help her reconnect with something joyful.

Mom had grown, too. She had struggled at first with my relationship with Erin, but in time, she saw what I saw: Erin brought balance to my life.

I wondered again if Dad would have accepted Erin. I told him, "You would have liked her. She's funny. And kind."

I knew his answer in my bones: "She's good for you."

In the quiet that followed, I noticed my breath: the way it caught, shallow and tight, just as it had for as long as I could remember. The repeated injuries to my nose culminating in a collapsed septum, my lifelong subconscious fear of not being able to breathe, and my fear of being silenced—the medicine finally helped me see that they were all connected.

Later, Alex passed by the fire pit. I heard him murmuring, "*Gracias Madre*. Thank you for the message. I got it. I got it. Message received."

There was reluctant acceptance in his voice—an almost sarcastic submission.

I suppressed the urge to laugh and say, "Congratulations, brother." It appeared I was not the only one learning a hard lesson.

I stayed in the temple to process for a long time after the closing. One thing was clear: I still had more to face.

Life has a way of taking us on a wild ride, only to bring us back to where we started. That's been true for me on several issues. Abortion is one of them.

My views have shifted completely over time. I went from hearing my birth mother say she was glad she hadn't had an abortion and vowing I'd never have one; to studying criminal justice and having my beliefs challenged by a professor who suggested that many people on the wrong side of the law were the products of unwanted pregnancies; to being in the position myself of feeling trapped and making an impossible choice.

And finally, decades later, to acknowledging it as a regret.

A few months later while traveling in France, I found myself in awe of a woman laid to rest at the Pantheon in Paris. Her name was Simone Veil, and she was a Holocaust survivor, a champion of women's rights, and the woman who helped legalize abortion in France. She knew women would seek it out regardless of the law, and that creating a legal and safe avenue would prevent more tragedy, not cause it. She once said, "No woman resorts to abortion with a light heart."

While now I wish I had made a different choice, I also recognize that not everyone's path is the same. Sometimes the last resort really is the only option. But I've come to believe that ending a life should never be the default, nor the "easy" answer, nor the first thought when hardship arises.

It's not about policy, it's about the inner landscape: the grief, the weight, and the scars no one sees that remain long after the decision is made and the deed is done. Maybe that's why I resisted grieving for so long—because to grieve would be to admit that something had been lost.

Healing is not moving on. It's learning to carry the weight of what can't be undone, with grace and forgiveness, and with love.

Before bed, I felt prompted to ask the staff at breakfast if they could find out from Inti or Rosalia what the oldest thing on the property might be. Later in the day, Rosie found me.

"Some trees behind your cabin," she said. "They're the oldest things here."

I wasn't sure why I had been invited to inquire, but I knew by now to follow the thread. I sauntered into the brush, tilting my head up to look through the dense canopy. The trees stood like elders—towering, thinning, some beginning to decay. Their time was nearing its end.

They reminded me of the signal trees in the Ozarks—living waypoints shaped by Indigenous hands long before I ever walked the land, before any fence was drawn or building raised. They carried the intentions of Osage hunters and Cherokee settlers, men and women who moved not just with purpose, but with reverence. The Osage knew those hills intimately, long before they were pushed west. The Cherokee, too, passed through, first as "Old Settlers," then again in sorrow during the Trail of Tears. That soil absorbed their songs, their prayers, their grief.

After a recent windstorm, a massive oak had fallen near my house. I was stunned to realize that it was a signal tree—one I'd never noticed, despite walking past it countless times. The bend was above eye level, and I'd simply never lifted my gaze.

According to my research, the signal trees, or marker trees, were at least 150 years old. Their gnarled, deliberate bends marked them as silent sentinels of a forgotten past, shaped with care and purpose. It was believed that they pointed to water, shelter, or gathering places. I often wondered about the hands that shaped them, the knowledge they carried in coded messages, the journeys that passed beneath their branches.

Whatever their purpose, I felt their presence, not as relics of history, but as guardians, rooted in time. Remnants of an ancient conversation between nature and man. A connection to the old ways.

I placed my hand on one of the old trees. "I see you," I whispered.

Months later, Inti showed me a photograph, a black and white image taken decades ago on the church property. Eight Seminole men were gathered around a small fire, surrounded by trees, their expressions solemn and timeless. I stared at their faces, wondering if their spirits were still on the land, watching and guiding.

CHAPTER 42
CRYSTALS AND COYOTES

"You are not the mistakes of your past. You are the wisdom of your healing." –Unknown

The fourth ceremony had been so taxing, it left me physically weak and emotionally drained for most of the following day. Had the fifth ayahuasca ceremony been scheduled for the next night, I'm not sure I would have had the strength.

Thankfully, the next day was a crystal ceremony, with each of us lying down on a bed of smooth, polished stones. I hoped their energy would restore what the previous night had depleted.

Rosalia gathered us outside the temple and explained that crystals hold a high frequency, capable of promoting healing and alignment. She guided me to a bed of amethyst crystals, their deep purple hue radiating quiet strength. Other stones were placed in my palms, on my abdomen, and on my forehead. I settled in to the soft, meditative music playing on a small speaker.

As it had during the ceremony in the little garden, energy shifted through my body, especially in my lower abdomen. However, it wasn't the same restless energy needing release. It was a soreness: a dull, aching sensation, like the tenderness left behind as an injury heals.

I focused on releasing any lingering negative energy into the sand beneath me. I allowed my body to sink into the crystals, imagining them drawing out whatever remained of my burdens.

When I rose twenty minutes later, I was a new woman. The weight I had been carrying—the exhaustion, the heaviness—was gone.

I stepped outside the temple and sat in a chair, gazing at the soft afternoon sky. Clouds were gathering—gentle, light gray formations against the pale blue. As I watched, an image emerged. A swaddled infant, sleeping peacefully in the golden light. Then I noticed a second infant facing the first. They were at peace. And finally, so was I.

Later, I met with Rosalia. She looked at me with knowing eyes. "This is why you were called to this retreat—to heal these wounds, to mend what remained unresolved with your own mothers, and your missed opportunity to be a mother."

She told me that genuine connection with Mother Earth is difficult when we carry conflict surrounding maternal relationships. She shared the story of another woman, also in her fifties, who had come to the church suffering from lifelong insomnia. She had tried everything. During one of her ceremonies, she was brought back to a long-buried memory: a pregnancy she had ended when she was a teenager. The spirit of the child came to her, reminding her of the name she had once chosen for it. Once she acknowledged it, and asked for forgiveness, the wound healed. She never had insomnia again.

Rosalia and I talked about the themes that had surfaced for me— suffocation, control, responsibility, forgiveness. I wondered if my physical injuries mirrored my emotional wounds. "We attract experiences that reflect our unresolved suffering," she said. "Nothing happens by accident."

She asked if I was ready for the final ceremony. I exhaled. "More so than before the crystal ceremony."

She smiled. "Perhaps this one will be gentle?"

Throughout the day, I reflected on why I had ended my pregnancies. Both times, I had told myself the timing wasn't right. But I knew that I had chosen convenience over responsibility. The truth had been waiting for me to claim it. This wasn't about punishment. It was about finally being honest with myself.

Later that afternoon, my mind wandered to something seemingly unrelated—the coyotes that had been encroaching on the house and were likely responsible for Rees's missing chickens and ducks.

Since purchasing the Middle Ground, I had refused to allow any predator hunting on the land. That included bears and coyotes. I wanted the land to be a refuge for wildlife. But now, with the coyotes growing bold enough to come near the house in broad daylight, I was torn.

I had a responsibility to protect life—my dogs, my cats, and the one remaining duck, Luna. Everyone I'd spoken to agreed: culling the coyotes was the only option. But I wasn't so sure.

As dusk approached, I closed my eyes and prayed.

"Mother Ayahuasca, I am open to receive. Let me come to fully understand the messages and lessons that have surfaced, and trust I can carry them into my daily life. With every step, I honor the path, trust the unfolding, and awaken to my purpose. Amen."

And with that, I stepped into the temple.

CHAPTER 43
FULL CIRCLE

"There is a voice that doesn't use words. Listen." — Rumi

A beautiful grove of trees unfolded before me, cloaked in darkness. It was nighttime, though the grove itself shimmered with its own quiet light. I began searching for a path. The trees stood tall and strong, but no direct route was visible. I considered cutting down a few to make a straighter path, but the idea was immediately offensive—viscerally wrong.

A slightly crooked route illuminated on the ground before me. With a little zig here and a little zag there, a playful path meandered through the grove, whimsical and lighthearted, gently nudging me toward an understanding: there are no straight paths in life. The twists and turns are how it's meant to be. Enjoy the journey. Welcome the unexpected.

Suddenly, the illuminated path transformed. Small wooden stakes emerged from the ground on either side. They were angled outward, creating a V-shaped channel. A gentle stream flowed down the path. It filled with water and became a river that ended where I stood.

From the back of the grove, something floated toward me. It was a basket, carried by the water. As it drifted closer, I could see something inside. A baby, swaddled in cloth: Moses. When he reached me, he evaporated into the air, dissolving into light as the water flowed through me. A sense of incredible peace settled over me—something had been delivered, carried to where it needed to go.

Tiny pink neon stingrays appeared in the water, giggling and joyful, like children playing in a stream. They piled up, too many for the narrow channel. I grew concerned. They needed more space. I had to save them. I carried them to the ocean and set them free.

A wave of déjà vu crashed over me. *What is that all about? Déjà vu?* I wondered.

A massive cat-like woman appeared. She sat on all fours, gazing down at a vast, suspended river that floated in the galaxy. She was huge, towering many times larger than a human, her presence almost Egyptian, like the statues who guard the grand temples of Luxor. Her sleek black skin was painted with fluorescent markings, glowing softly in the darkness. She wore a mischievous grin, exuding both power and playfulness.

I looked at the floating river before her—countless shimmering strands, parallel universes stretched across time. I watched as, with a single clawed fingertip, she reached out and flicked the strands ever so slightly. She was shifting reality. Crossing timelines. Causing moments to overlap, just enough for us to sense it.

"That's a little cruel," I teased.

Her grin widened. "It's all in good fun."

The gentle sound of rain pulled my awareness back to the temple. I had a strong desire to let the rain wash over me. Outside, the rain was cool and soft, falling in gentle waves at first. Then the drizzle became a downpour. I laughed, feeling my clothes soak up the water, letting it cleanse my body and mind.

Now a pair of electrical wire cutters appeared, standing upright on the ground before me. *You want me to become an electrician?* I stared at the cutters, trying to understand. Doing wiring on the building had not given me a strong desire to pursue it further.

Electricity flows inside the walls, through ceilings, under floors. It joins with other wires and forms junctions. If a wire becomes disconnected or broken, the system fails. Energy cannot reach its intended destination until the damage is repaired. Like faulty wiring in a house, my inner systems had needed rewiring. Ayahuasca had shown me where the breaks were.

Chaos erupted around me. Alex was yelling at God again. Others were crying, purging, battling their demons, but I was calm.

"If your house is wired correctly," She said, "you don't need to be pulled into other people's storms. Hold space, but let them do their own repairs. Be an example for others."

"Okay," I replied, feeling a weighty question. "Whose example should *I* follow?"

Her response came softly. "Jesus is a good example."

For a moment, I froze, the simplicity and truth of it settling deep in my bones. It had been there all along—an answer that I'd resisted, but that now felt undeniable.

"Okay," I whispered, humbled. "Okay."

The clouds were gone, and moonlight streamed in through the side of the temple, casting a silvery glow.

The sun is demanding, expecting effort, pushing us to be productive. The moon asks for nothing in return as She recharges everything with a soft, loving presence.

"Thank you," I whispered. "Thank you for always being a guiding force in my life. A quiet companion through the years."

"Do I need more sacrament?" I asked.

"No. This is a good place to stop."

I focused on the lyrics to the music that was playing in the temple. It was about breathing and flowing with the rhythm of the Universe. I noticed that I was gently rocking on my mat, as I always did in the medicine.

"Stop trying to create your own rhythm," She told me. "Flow with the rhythm of the Universe."

I stopped rocking and felt a wave of pure, clean energy flow through me. It traveled down all the wires of my house and filled me with a sense of tranquility.

After a ceremony, my mind was usually too busy unraveling what had happened for my stomach to be anything but revolted at the thought of food. But for once, I was actually hungry.

On the porch, we laughed and shared stories. We'd each weathered private storms. Now, we shared a meal as laughter filled the silence that once held grief.

Rosalia joined the conversation, her presence as grounding as ever. I told her that during the first ceremony she had blown my mind when she said to me, "Remember who you are." She had no memory of saying it. She smiled. "That happens a lot. Sometimes, I feel prompted to say something. I don't always know why."

It was confirmation that she wasn't merely guiding the ceremonies— she was tuning into something greater and trusting it to speak through her.

I asked her how she had come to be a spiritual leader. She laughed, then shared her own transformation—the story of a young woman who had been looking for one thing and found something much greater. She had sought out ayahuasca hoping only for relief from personal trauma, but as her heart healed, she discovered a calling to serve others.

CHAPTER 44
VISION OR ILLUSION

"We do not see things as they are, we see them as we are." –
Anaïs Nin

In the morning I drove north to Arlington, Virginia, and a flight to
France to catch up with Erin. I should have been exhausted, but I felt
alive—clear-headed and full of energy.

Along the way, I stopped in Richmond, Virginia, to visit my college
roommate Mindy. When I pulled into her driveway, I was met by an
enormous Central Asian Shepherd I didn't recognize as one of hers.
The dog looked like she could tear me apart.

I put my hand out for her to sniff. She checked me out, decided I was
not a threat, and pressed her nose against my hand. She looked up at
me with a gentle no-nonsense expression. No fear or aggression, just
quiet trust. I scratched behind her ears as Mindy stepped out onto the
porch to greet me.

"That's Nadya. She belongs to my neighbor. She's terrified of storms and jumps the fence looking for a place to hide."

Mindy told me Nadya's owner planned to euthanize her, having decided she wasn't cut out for livestock work. Mindy took Nadya gently by the collar and led her back to the field where her sheep awaited.

Something in my gut twisted at the thought of such a gentle giant being put down for convenience. I prayed, "Divine Spirit, Please help Nadya find a new home."

An immediate response came: "I just did."

Damn it. Erin was going to kill me. The last thing we needed was another dog. I had recently taken on two Pyrenees Coon-hound mix puppies, Newton and Nona. I had intended for it to be only one puppy and "accidentally" ended up with litter-mates. Also, instead of being outside guard dogs patrolling the farm at night, they were sleeping in bed with me. Epic fail.

I already knew Nadya was coming to the Ozarks. Fortunately, she was also an answer to a problem. She was already an outdoor dog, a guardian. She needed a place where she had a job, shelter from storms, and no fences to trap her. She could hide safe and warm under our porch, and keep the coyotes away from the chickens and Luna the duck.

I could save her life, and in return, she could save theirs—and the coyotes.

When Mindy returned, I pitched the idea. She called her neighbor, and just like that, the decision was made.

When I returned from France, I'd have one minor detour, and one giant dog.

It wasn't the easy choice. It was the right choice.

When I arrived in France and began telling Erin about the ceremonies, she listened quietly, then asked, "But how do you know it's real? Isn't it just a psychedelic hallucination? Something you want to believe?" Classic Erin: the grounded one. The anchor I don't always appreciate in the moment.

It's a fair question. I had asked myself the same thing. After all, the mind is a master of illusion. Dreams can trick us. Mugwort tea had led me into a dream so real I wondered if it had actually happened. But ayahuasca didn't feel like fantasy. It felt like precision. Not chaos, but clarity.

Ayahuasca quieted the part of my mind that clung to identity, to certainty, to control. She allowed me to find myself beneath the noise. She allowed my soul the chance to speak freely that it had been waiting for.

When Brad had described his single experience as "ten years of therapy in four hours," I had thought he was exaggerating. I no longer felt that way.

Hallucinations come and go, but the lessons learned through ayahuasca stayed. Since beginning this path, I'd been waking to birdsong instead of panic. My jaw had unclenched. The tightness I often felt in my chest was gone.

Recently, on a flight back to the Ozarks, I had been selected once again for additional TSA screening. Something in my bag had caught the attention of the agent reviewing the X-ray. I stepped to the side and opened my backpack for inspection.

What struck me wasn't the inconvenience; it was the absence of any detectable reaction inside my body. No heat rising in my chest. No spike in heart rate. No flash of indignation. I was calm, inside and out.

I had stopped drinking altogether. In some ways, I missed it. There were nights when I actually wanted to have a glass of wine with dinner.

I'd feel a nostalgic pull and tell Erin, "Pour me a splash." But time after time, the taste on my lips made my stomach turn. Eventually, I accepted that I no longer had a relationship with alcohol. Thankfully, that acceptance also smoothed away the awkwardness in social situations that had so often driven me to drink just to loosen up.

I asked Erin if she thought I had changed.

She said that I was easier to talk to now. That in the past, she'd worried about being honest with me because she feared I would shut down. That she'd learned to choose her words carefully, or not say things at all. She pointed out that we'd relied on alcohol as a crutch to speak our minds to each other.

She reminded me of a fight we'd had in May of 2022, during a house-hunting trip to Orlando. The trip was memorable not because of the chaotic Florida housing market at the time, with homes renting within hours of being listed, but because it marked the first real fight of our marriage.

After two bottles of wine at the hotel, a conversation long overdue finally broke open. Everything we were carrying spilled out at once: the stress of parenting a teen who had already endured enough trauma for a lifetime, endless fertility injections and heartbreak, and pandemic pandemonium leading me down a rabbit hole of hyper-vigilance and paranoia, convinced the world was closing in on me.

Erin told me she wasn't sure I was a very good parent anyway, and that maybe it had all worked out for the best. The comment cut deeply, and I shut down completely. For the next couple of days, I withdrew, said very little, and carried the hurt in silence. We hadn't talked about it again.

Now, we did. Calmly, without defensiveness, and without triggers. Without tears or escalation. We spoke about it as if it were water under the bridge—something that had happened, something that had hurt, and something that no longer held power over us.

Erin pointed out that this very conversation—that we could revisit something deeply painful and simply communicate openly, without fear and without the "assistance" of alcohol—was evidence of change.

She also told me that she'd been angry, scared, and embarrassed more than once when I'd had one too many.

As she said it, I flashed back to a night in 2021, when I hit rock bottom and seriously considered ending my life because I couldn't see a way forward.

I had stormed out of the house, drunk and furious, terrified of losing everything I had spent my life building: my career, my identity, my purpose. I was headed to the bar, but I didn't make it far before I collapsed. With nowhere to run from the pressure, I buried my head in my hands and contemplated whether a life no longer mine was worth living.

The mandate wasn't just a policy. It represented a lack of freedom, autonomy, and consent. It was a line in the sand that declared that unless I fell in line, my years of service, sacrifice, and loyalty didn't matter to the system I had served. The loss of agency, erosion of trust, and pressure to submit—to betray my conscience—nearly broke me.

Eventually the Mexican police found me and used my phone to call Erin to come collect me off the sidewalk.

I wondered why that night had never surfaced in ceremony. Then again, maybe it had—just not in a way I could recognize at the time. Healing doesn't always come in visions. Sometimes it comes later, when we're ready to live what we've learned. Erin had not only been a witness to that pain, she had lived it too—the need for healing wasn't mine alone.

Reflecting on that night made me realize how far I had come, and gave me a deep appreciation for how much I loved my life: Erin, our little family with Danni and a growing gaggle of dogs, the land in the

Ozarks, a renewed pull to walk the Camino, and a new sense of purpose that was finally beginning to take shape.

I was learning to listen to both my body and my spirit. For the first time in a long time, I felt in alignment: my relationships were more honest, my priorities more grounded, my love of life restored, and my connection to the Divine renewed.

If that was all an illusion, I decided, I was okay with that.

CHAPTER 45
SAINTE GENEVIÈVE

"Prayer is when you talk to God. Intuition is when God talks to you." –Dr. Wayne Dyer

---

As Erin and I explored Paris, I unexpectedly found myself face to face with my hometown.

Sainte Geneviève, Missouri, was settled by the French in the 1700s. History was carved into those limestone buildings on the banks of the Mississippi River. But it wasn't until I found myself inside Notre Dame that I learned Sainte Geneviève was the patron saint of Paris, a woman who faced destruction and did not give in to fear. When Attila the Hun threatened to burn the city to the ground, she didn't flee. She didn't prepare for war. She prayed, she fasted, and she convinced the people of Paris not to abandon their city.

In the end, Attila turned away. Paris was spared.

I stood in front of the small chapel bearing her name, absorbing the story of a woman whose greatest weapon had been faith.

For years, I had tried to be tough. For so much of my life, I had believed that action kept you safe, that meaning came from struggle, and that justice required force. But here was a woman who had saved an entire city without ever picking up a weapon.

For too long, I had lived by a code that told me everything worth having had to be fought for, that power meant control, and that security meant always being ready for battle. And yet, the greatest transformation of my life had come not from force, but from listening to something greater than myself.

Now here I stood in Paris, thousands of miles from where I was born, looking at the name I had carried with me proudly my entire life: "I am from Sainte Geneviève."

The name had always been there. The meaning had taken time to reveal itself.

Erin and I continued moving through the cathedral of Notre Dame until I paused in front of another chapel. It wasn't particularly striking. Unlike the others, it had no statues, no ornate decorations—only an abstract painting on the wall with dark blue hues like stormy seas. There was nothing that should have drawn me in. And yet I stood there, unable to move forward.

Erin, well versed in my journey, looked at me. "Does this chapel call to you?"

I hesitated. "Yeah. I don't know. I guess."

She chuckled and pointed to a small sign I hadn't noticed, which read, "Chapel of Moses."

Moses. The man who had first entered my thoughts on a rare lazy afternoon, then surfaced in visions, in symbols, in books, in moments of synchronicity that were impossible to ignore.

I dropped some coins in the donation box, lit a candle, and sat down in a nearby chair. I closed my eyes. *Why was I prompted to stop here? Why Moses?*

I sat in silence, waiting. The answer came. Because Moses was reluctant when called. Moses questioned his own worthiness. He doubted, hesitated, even asked someone else to be sent instead.

As I sat in Notre Dame, watching the priests in white robes consecrate the Eucharist—turning the bread and the wine into the body and blood of Christ—I felt something familiar. Not in the ritual itself, but in the intention behind it.

It may sound like a contradiction to criticize organized religion one moment and stand in awe at a cathedral the next. But Notre Dame moved me not because of its ties to one of the most hierarchical religions in the world, but because something divine lingers in places built with love, devotion, and intention.

In that sacred space, I could recognize the sincerity of those around me. For many, this was their path to the Divine—their way of seeking truth, comfort, and connection. Who was I to say it was any less valid than the path I'd found in a simple wooden temple in South Florida?

That moment in Notre Dame solidified something: my journey was not about rejecting religion. It was about reclaiming the right to seek the Divine on our own terms, and recognizing that whether we find God in a cathedral, a mosque, a sweat lodge, a synagogue, the jungle, or the forest, what matters is not the location, but the sincerity of the seeker.

The burning bush that had called to Moses set him on a path he had never imagined for himself: a path he doubted, feared, and tried to avoid. But he answered the call anyway. Sitting there, next to the Chapel of Moses, directly across the nave from the Chapel of Sainte Geneviève, I saw my own hesitation reflected back to me: my reluctance to step fully into what I was being called to do, to surrender and allow myself to be led. I decided then and there that I would not let fear stop me. I would stop hesitating and embrace a new chapter with an open heart, even when it would be easier to retreat and re-armor.

We left Notre Dame and ducked into a café for coffee and crêpes. As we were gathering our things, a local man approached us, randomly and unsolicited.

"You know," he said, pointing toward the street behind us, "you can see the Panthéon from here."

"What's the Panthéon?" I asked Erin, my go-to history buff.

She wasn't sure. A quick search revealed it was originally a church dedicated to Sainte Geneviève, at one time her resting place, and now a secular mausoleum. The synchronicity was impossible to dismiss.

After visiting the Panthéon and paying our respects to Sainte Geneviève, Simone Veil, and others deemed to have led a life worthy enough to be entombed there, we continued wandering through the streets where history lived and breathed.

Paris was full of old churches, but one in the Latin Quarter caught our attention: Saint-Nicolas du Chardonnet, a 13th-century church with towering stone walls. As we were leaving, two women spoke to Erin in French, inviting us the next day for Mass. And not just any Mass—a Latin Mass, the old way, unchanged by time. It was a chance to witness Catholic devotion as it was closer to the beginning.

We returned the next morning at 10:00 a.m. I didn't understand a word of the Mass, and yet I loved it. It didn't matter that I wasn't Catholic or that I didn't know when to stand or kneel. I wasn't there as a tourist. My intentions were pure.

I closed my eyes and let the Gregorian chants wash over me—absorbing them more in my bones than in my ears. For those moments, I was in some other time and place.

A jolt of déjà vu swept over me. I almost laughed out loud, picturing the cat-lady of my parallel-universe theory plucking at the strings of my existence and shifting puzzle pieces for her own entertainment.

In front of us sat three generations of women, a modern-day scene from my vision of the ancestors: grandmother, mother, and granddaughter, if their strong resemblance was any indication.

The little girl was maybe five. She sat through the entire service without a sound. Near the end, when the congregation kneeled, she remained in her seat until her mother grabbed her arm and pulled her down firmly.

I wondered whether she would grow into her faith, or spend forty years searching for something she couldn't name, because she'd never been given the chance to choose it for herself. Would my relationship with God and religion have been different if I hadn't felt so oppressed by it as a young woman?

Then again, I don't know that I'd change a single thing.

CHAPTER 46

THE LONG ROAD BACK TO EACH OTHER

"It is not time that heals all wounds. It is love." –Unknown

On our way to the train station to leave Paris, "L.O.V.E." by Nat King Cole came on the radio in the Uber. It's one of Erin's favorite songs to sing, and one of my favorites to hear her sing. The melody filled the car, a quiet reminder that the road ahead would be paved in love.

Love had been the overarching theme of every conversation I'd had with Mother Ayahuasca: love for self, for others, for plants, for animals, and for the Earth.

I've seen what it looks like when pain hollows people out; when the wounds of war, of violence, of loss, leave nothing but echoes. I'd seen it in others, and I'd carried it in myself.

Ayahuasca stripped away everything I had used to stay numb. She showed me what I'd buried, and asked me to sit with it.

In all the searching I had done, one thing remained at the core of everything: love. It was love that kept me searching for meaning. Love broke me open. Love guided me toward healing. Yet for so much of my life, I misunderstood it.

I had seen love as something earned. I spent years believing that if I worked hard enough, fought hard enough, gave enough, became enough, I would be worthy of it. I had known unconditional love from my father, yet after he passed, I found myself questioning whether he would have still accepted me after I stepped fully into who I was.

Now I mourned the girl who believed she had to earn the right to be held, who believed that love was a ledger to be balanced.

I began to finally accept that I never had anything to prove, or to earn. Because love—real love—is given, not traded. It is recognized, not rewarded. It does not arrive because we deserve it. It arrives because we are.

Most of all, I was no longer angry, and that made me easier to love. I was allowing myself to be loved.

Erin saw the changes in me before I understood them myself. At first, she was cautiously optimistic. She had always known me as fiercely independent, strong-willed, and someone who rarely looked back once wronged.

I had once worried about us growing apart because of my spiritual journey, but our individual paths brought us into closer alignment. Cancer led Erin to do her own reorganization. Now she was also skipping wine with dinner and choosing the healthier menu option. Her path bent toward mine, from a crisis toward healing.

One afternoon, as I sat at my desk surrounded by notes and half-formed thoughts, she asked me how I knew that my work was a calling and not just an idea.

I said, "I think when it won't leave you alone—when you feel compelled to follow it even when it's hard, even when you'd rather not —that's when it's more than an idea."

Then Erin told me something that made my heart swell: she'd been wondering if her own lifelong tug to pursue a law degree might be her own calling. Another step toward alignment, not of our specific paths, but of our desire to find and follow the threads drawing us forward. As it turns out, having different paths doesn't mean that we aren't on the journey together.

From Paris, I flew into Washington, D.C., and made the detour to collect Nadya. Then I plugged in my destination and headed for the Ozarks. I didn't overthink it; I just hit the gas and drove west. I didn't check which route my GPS recommended—something that concerns Erin every time, considering my aforementioned navigational challenges.

So when the GPS took me through St. Louis, within an hour of my mom, I took it as a sign. I got to her place at four in the morning and asked her to come with me for a few days. After some coaxing, she agreed. As Mom, Nadya, and I made the final turn onto my dirt road, I stepped out to open the gate—and froze.

A large brown-and-white owl was perched low in a tree, just off the road, calm and still. Its knowing eyes locked onto mine, unbothered by my arrival.

I stood still, breath held. After a moment, the owl lifted into the air on its silent wings and disappeared into the forest.

I lingered a moment longer. When I had first set foot on this land over two decades earlier, I'd been greeted by an owl—not in form, but in spirit. Now one had shown up in the flesh, as if to welcome me home.

Rees and I had planned a surprise fishing trip, but the weather turned cold and windy. We improvised with breakfast at a local diner and antique shopping. Over bacon and eggs, Mom started telling stories about her childhood, mine, and Rees's.

She talked about fishing trips with her dad and how, as much as she loved them, her favorite part was stopping for breakfast, "At a diner like this one," she said.

I asked if it would be okay to share our story—the truth of where we'd struggled and how we'd found our way back to each other. She hesitated, then said yes. She cried as she told me she had done the best she could—but she believed she had failed.

She explained that when she and Dad moved to Missouri from Utah, she had no support system. Money was tight. That was why only Dad had traveled to pick me up from the hospital. When he came home with a three-day-old baby, she had to figure it out on her own.

She told me how they had prayed and prayed for a child. "You were an answer to our prayers," she said.

We laughed about how her mother had sent lacy dresses that I refused to wear.

I asked, "And there was never a conversation between you and Dad about why I didn't like dresses or dolls?"

"No," she replied honestly.

Fair enough. It was a question I had been wanting to ask, and now I had. She told me that when she was growing up, being in "a situation like yours" wasn't just frowned upon. It was considered wrong.

She said she could see how much happier I was with Erin, and how I was able to be my true self. She told me that she never liked my ex-husband and thought he was a bully. She had said nothing because she didn't think it was her place, but it was hard to watch me with someone who was not right for me.

It was a moment of growth for both of us. She didn't need to understand everything. She only needed to care that I was happy, and she did.

I told her I was proud of her—for being willing to change, to see differently than she had been taught. To choose love over dogma.

She told me she knew that she worried about everything. It was in her nature. She had inherited it from her mother, who grew up during the Great Depression and lost her father in a mine explosion and her two-year-old sister to pneumonia. Grandma had eaten watercress and onion sandwiches as a young girl. No wonder she worried.

Trauma doesn't just shape a generation. It echoes forward until someone stops it.

I told her I knew she had done her best and that it was perfect in its own way. "I love you," I said, then added sincerely, "Some of my best qualities came from you."

She told me that everything I'd done in my life had scared her. When I became a police officer, she was terrified. I don't remember this, but she said that one day I called and asked, "Dad, did you pray for me today?"

"Yes," he'd replied. "I pray for you every day."

Then I told them about the shooting. This did not improve her tendency to worry.

As I learned to let fear go—to stop letting it run my life—I began to see how much it had always ruled hers. She still lived from that place. Every thought seemed filtered through danger, every choice weighed against what might go wrong.

"Be careful driving in the rain—traffic accidents. Don't go anywhere crowded—terrorists. Don't hike in the woods—bears. Don't travel in winter—snow and ice."

It was endless. Don't go, don't risk, don't live, because you could die. As I learned to see that fear for what it was, recognizing it, and then ignoring it, became easier. It was liberating.

As we talked throughout the day and into the night, we healed old wounds. We had conversations that were decades overdue. She tearfully told me how hurt she had been when Dad helped me track down my birth mother in high school without including her. She had found the letters in my room and felt deeply betrayed by both of us. When she became overcome with emotion, I crossed the room and put my arms around her. I told her our intent had been to protect her, not to hurt her. We cried together, the weight of years lifting.

In my twenties, I also met my birth father. My adoptive father went along with me, and we had lunch at a quiet Japanese restaurant. They had both walked the streets of Japan as Mormon missionaries, just a few years apart, preaching the same gospel.

At the time, I didn't fully realize the gift that moment offered. These two men spoke easily: the one who raised me, and the one who gave me life. And I was there, not as a secret or a sin, but just as myself.

Most of the time, reconciliation doesn't come with fireworks or perfect words. Sometimes, it's a quiet meal, a gentle meeting, and a reminder that complicated pasts don't have to define our futures.

If my mother's view on something she once saw as wrong could shift so dramatically, what else might society be wrong about? What truths are we refusing to see because they challenge what we were taught? History is full of beliefs we had to outgrow. Maybe the stigma around plant medicine is one of them.

Change doesn't come from force. It comes from love and from ordinary people being willing to think for themselves. When enough people are brave enough to question what they were taught, when love and truth outlast fear, that's when change will come. Mom reminded me of that. And if she could change, maybe we all could.

Months later, I finally picked up the phone and called my birth mother. We hadn't spoken in more than twenty years. A few emails here and there, but that heavy silence had never broken open.

Her voice was soft and welcoming as she told me more about the circumstances of my birth. She had gotten her first and only flu shot while pregnant with me, to convince her mother to get one. Afterward, she became gravely ill with Sjögren's disease. Her weight dropped to ninety pounds and she couldn't eat.

Doctors told her she had six months to live, and that the baby likely wouldn't survive. They spent three months trying to convince her to terminate the pregnancy.

"I figured, if I was going to die anyway, I might as well roll the dice for you." She paused, then added, "You were not supposed to live. And you were born healthy. You were a miracle."

She continued, "They aren't always right. They were wrong about you. And about me. We both lived."

In awe, I replied, "Wow. What an impossible choice. Thank you." Now I knew where I got my courage and defiance of the experts.

I told her I'd like to visit, and she said she would love that. I told her I'd written about her—about how our paths had diverged and how much her story had shaped mine. I joked that I must've gotten the writing bug from her, since I knew she'd published a few books of her own.

"Fair warning. It's a brutally honest account of my life, and mistakes."

She didn't flinch. "Those are the best kind."

When we hung up, I wondered why I'd put off that conversation for so long.

CHAPTER 47
THE BISON

"In every walk with nature one receives far more than he seeks."
–John Muir

One day while working on the building, I pulled up to the site, parked my truck, stepped out, and found a massive, majestic bison staring me down. I blinked. I wasn't in ceremony. This was real.

We looked at each other. Then he turned and barreled down the cleared path we'd dug for the water line. When he reached the main road, he took a left and headed south, disappearing into the trees.

After taking a stunned minute to absorb the sacredness of meeting a bison face to face, I sent a message to Inti, along with a video I was fortunate enough to capture. The bison had paused in his charge through the woods, looking back just long enough that my video caught the unmistakable curve of his horns.

Inti wrote, "The Tatanka does not appear by coincidence." He said that maybe the bison came as an affirmation, a blessing—a reminder that I was on a path of healing, protection, and purpose.

He sent me a Lakota song, a traditional chant used to call the bison. I walked to the meditation pond still under construction behind the building, and sat on a rock next to a concrete angel. I pressed play and let the melody wash over me, filling my eyes with tears.

During the winter retreat, the marker trees on my land had been part of my vision. The Chief, the message to find the oldest thing on the land, the black-and-white photo of Seminole Indians—perhaps taken in the very spot on the church property I'd explored—all felt like more than a coincidence. They felt like a convergence.

Inti wrote, "Perhaps this isn't just about Native American traditions. Maybe it's something greater, more ancient. Part of a higher plan."

I told him that just the day before, I had written about the marker trees and their reminder that we're meant to carry the wisdom of the ancients forward.

Inti replied, "It is no coincidence that you are the guardian of that land. Honor that calling."

Could I have been drawn to this land because it has a spiritual energy, vibrating with the frequency of prayer across lifetimes? One morning after ceremony, I awoke thinking about reincarnation. What if I was drawn to this path not out of curiosity, but because my soul remembered it? For me, ayahuasca had felt not like a discovery, but a return.

Some months later, I saw the bison again. I was leaving the construction site, and as I rounded the corner onto the country road, there he was, walking nonchalantly down the middle of the road toward me.

I put my truck in park and rolled down the window. "Hey, buddy," I said as he passed the open window, his massive head swinging slightly with each step. He didn't stop—just kept walking, calm and unbothered. When he reached the drive, he paused, looked down the driveway toward the building, then continued on past the property and out of sight.

As he ambled away slowly, without fear, I opened Spotify and played the Lakota "Call of the Buffalo" song Inti had sent me. I'm not sure, but I think he liked it.

A few weeks later, I had the unexpected opportunity to be close to the Church during a farewell Disney trip before moving overseas with Erin for work.

It was the first one-night ceremony I'd attended since that first time, when I'd failed to connect with the Divine despite drinking five cups of sacrament.

On this trip, I had no such fears. I felt the kind of kinship and camaraderie that I had once believed were not possible outside of military and law-enforcement circles. It turns out that those bonds come from dedicating your lives to a shared purpose.

My visions flowed easily between the present, past, and future. I saw many sad souls walking through the woods on my property in the Ozarks. They walked alone among the trees, beginning the journey of self-discovery and forgiveness, the long healing process of taking responsibility for their pasts.

My thoughts turned again to the marker trees, particularly the one that had come down near the house. I was still unsure of the right way to recognize or honor them, their purpose, and all they had witnessed.

I sometimes wonder if, in our care not to overstep into traditions that aren't ours, we risk letting their heritage fade away. Who twisted those trees, making them into shapes that stand out to others walking through the forest? Could they have been bent by young Osage or

Cherokee boys experimenting, unaware of how their actions would endure? Were they simply formed as a place to stop and rest, safely off the forest floor? Or, as many suggest, and I believe, were they bent to point the way toward shelter, water, or a meeting place? Whatever the reason, it seems likely the trees were intended to outlast the twisters.

When I carry a pouch of tobacco and pause at a signal tree—placing my hand on it, thanking it for bearing witness, and leaving an offering—I hope it is received in the spirit of respect. My intent is to honor the ones who walked this land long before I became its steward.

Even my name makes me wonder: did my father cross into appropriation, or was it simply one man's attempt to honor a culture he came to love?

I've come to believe that reverence matters more than bloodline, and that spiritual inheritance is not something we possess; it's something we return to. Plants are not confined by passports or pedigrees. They belong to the Earth, to the Divine—and we are all children of the Divine.

Could I give the fallen signal tree a new purpose? Make it into a bench and place it at a crossroads as a spot for seekers to stop, rest, and reflect? Maybe it doesn't matter which direction the elbow points, or what it once pointed toward, but simply that we pause to consider where our journey leads—especially when we think we are lost. That we consider what our ancestors would want us to do and to know. That we consider how to honor and respect them and each other.

Mother Ayahuasca asked, "If you saw someone taking a path you believed was wrong for them, would you try to course-correct them?"

She was reminding me of my tendency to "help" others, believing I "know better." She reminded me, as She had done at the winter retreat: "Just be a good example."

Everyone must stand at their own crossroads and choose their own path. All I, or anyone, can do is offer a place to pause and reflect.

It was a beautiful and gentle ceremony. Perhaps Mother Ayahuasca is gentler with me now, because I have learned to be gentle with myself.

CHAPTER 48

THE WEDDING AND THE WARRIOR

"No human laws are of any validity, if contrary to the law of nature." –Sir William Blackstone

---

I stayed on the church property the following day and night. In the morning, I was honored to witness the wedding of two members—an intimate gathering presided over by Inti. There wasn't a dry eye in the temple as two beautiful souls united to begin a life together.

Rosalia told them they only needed two things for a successful marriage: loyalty and communication. Then she added, with a smile, "Ayahuasca helps with the communication."

In the afternoon, I helped prepare the temple for the next ceremony, sweeping away the last of the footprints. A calmness spread over me, my breath syncing with the slow, steady rhythm of the broom. The simple act of gratitude left me feeling lighter.

That evening over dinner, Inti, Rosalia, Rosie, and I shared stories from our respective journeys. Lessons learned the hard way, laughter earned the honest way. The air was soft with the kind of ease that only comes when trust runs deep. We sat long after the meal was finished, letting the conversation drift naturally.

Inti asked if I had a photo of myself from my war-zone days. I pulled one up on my phone from my six-week ATLAS (Advanced Tactics Leadership and Skills) training before departing for Iraq in 2006. I am holding a .50-caliber machine gun, standing upright with a weapon designed to be mounted to a turret due to its size and recoil. I'm wearing a do-rag, cargo pants, body armor, t-shirt, and combat boots. A belt of ammo hangs from the gun. The photo is perfectly timed to catch a tracer round as it leaves the barrel, giving the illusion that the weapon is shooting fire. It's a pretty badass photo, if I do say so myself.

Inti looked at it in amazement, "Wow! You are not that same hard woman."

"No," I replied with a deep breath. I pointed toward the fire pit, the place where I had purged so much pain and shed my ego. "That woman is out there."

"Do you still remember that woman?" asked Rosie.

"Yes, I remember her. She was one of the boys for over twenty-five years. I wouldn't trade a minute of it."

Smiling, I added, "I remember her with pride. The badge will always be a part of my story. But today, I move through the world with a vine in my heart, peace in my soul, and no need for 'creds' to know who I am."

I shared with Rosalia my plans to write this book, and my concerns for the privacy of the CELDV community. I was also scared of losing my own anonymity. Once this story was out, there would be no taking it back.

Rosalia didn't hesitate. She looked at me across the table, her eyes kind as always. "When I first saw you," she said, "the warrior—I never imagined I would come to love you so much, or feel so close to you." Then she asked, "Has ayahuasca changed your life?"

"Yes," I told her, "It has changed everything."

She nodded. "Then think of how many people like you need to hear about it."

The following morning, I walked the church grounds with Inti. The sun was reaching its peak, filtering through the canopy in bright, golden shafts.

Years ago, I had walked my own land with a spiritual man who tried to speak to me about God, and I recoiled. I wasn't ready. Now, I walked sacred ground with a spiritual leader and spoke of God not with resistance, but with reverence.

We paused near a stretch of pines where the ground stayed soft year-round and the air smelled like earth and old rain. One of the trees had a bend low in the trunk, not dramatic, but enough to catch the eye. I ran my hand along the bark. "I've always been drawn to trees that find a way to survive despite the harsh conditions that shape them."

Inti gave a quiet smile and said nothing.

As we wandered through the grove, we talked about a future where ayahuasca could be shared freely, without fear of punishment or reprisal. A world where spiritual sovereignty is protected by law; where religious freedom is not only a founding ideal, it is a national ethos. A world where spiritual healing is not hidden, and connection to the Divine is not treated as a crime.

"I still can't believe that what we do here, what transformed my life, is illegal in most of this country," I said. "I used to think risk and illegality were the same thing. But alcohol nearly wrecked my life. Ayahuasca brought me back."

I gazed into the forest. "For twenty-six years, I served as a sworn law enforcement officer. I upheld the law. I believed in service and the rule of law. I still do. But that system criminalizes the plants God put on Earth to heal us. I don't know why I never questioned that. I had no idea this path existed."

Inti simply said, "Little by little." It was a phrase he used often, his way of saying that day by day, we will get there.

I continued, "I watched drugs destroy people I loved. Heroin robbed my brother of his potential. That reinforced what I'd been told all my life: drugs are bad and the laws are just. But not all substances are equal. Not all laws reflect justice."

Inti turned his gaze toward me. "So now you walk both paths?"

I nodded. "I haven't rejected the laws I once swore to uphold. I've only recognized that they currently deny healing, even to the very people who enforce them. Perhaps I can serve as a bridge between these communities. I no longer wear a badge, but the calling to serve others remains."

"So, you've found the Middle Ground?" He grinned. "Maybe the laws will soon change," he added hopefully. "This sacrament is older than the law. The law will catch up."

"I hope you're right." I laughed softly. "After all, who would've ever thought a retired federal agent and diplomat would become an ambassador for ayahuasca?"

AFTERWORD

"The noblest question in the world is: What good may I do in the world today?" –Benjamin Franklin

For years, a framed photo sat on my desk: a lone dog walking a wooded trail. The caption read, "Not all who wander are lost."

It stayed with me throughout my postings to various countries. I don't know where I first picked it up, and I know the phrase is well known, but the message always felt like it was for me. I wandered—God knows I wandered—but I was never truly lost. Even when I didn't know what I believed, I knew where home was: not a place, but a rhythm. A truth beneath all the noise.

As this book goes to print, I am in the final stages of preparation for Nona's Way—a 780-kilometer pilgrimage along the Camino de Santiago, with my dog Nona at my side. It is the walk I had hoped to take when I retired, but foot surgery forced a delay—and gave me time to walk a different kind of path first.

Now, I walk not to escape my past, but to honor it. Not to find myself, but to offer something back. Nona's Way is a walk for mental health and trauma recovery in the first responder community: a way to show that healing is possible, even when the road is hard. It's a walk to honor those still carrying invisible wounds, and those who lost the battle before they found help.

I wrote to my nephews and extended an olive branch, asking for forgiveness for any hurt or pain I'd caused and expressing a desire to reconnect. Whether they take me up on the offer or not, I sincerely hope they can find healing and a path toward releasing any anger they carry.

My relationship with Danni continues to improve. She visits us when she has breaks from school, and we enjoy our time together. She is healing in her own way and in her own time, and I could not be more proud of her.

Nadya quickly settled into her role as protector of the home and livestock. Nothing gets by her that isn't supposed to be there. She only barks when she has something to say, and there is no mistaking who is in charge when she does. Sadly, Luna the duck, born on the lunar eclipse, was lost to the coyotes a few days before I returned with Nadya.

Erin hasn't felt the pull to drink the sacrament, and that's okay. Our journey continues in its own rhythm. Her cancer changed us both, bringing our lives into focus, and forcing us to reckon with things we'd left ignored and unsaid. It showed us what really mattered.

I continue to nurture the seed that was planted at the WIFLE awards ceremony and to feel blessed that my ability to serve didn't have to end when the badge came off.

The new building is nearly complete, and I'm listening—letting the land guide what it becomes.

I'm planning to plant a weeping mulberry for Amel: a quiet, living tribute to her memory. Her name means "hope" in Arabic, and I like to believe that's what will take root here. Everything changes. Everything moves.

Maybe that's all this journey ever was—learning how to see the signs, how to listen, how to let things become what they're meant to be. As I sit here, surrounded by the land that continues to teach me, I know the journey isn't over.

The vine that once cracked me open now roots me into something ancient and alive.

ACKNOWLEDGMENTS

To Mother Ayahuasca, who called to me and conspired with the Universe so that I could answer.

And to the ancestors—those who walked the forests long before me and left markers for those willing to pause and listen—thank you for guiding me home.

To Centro Espiritualista Luz Do Vegetal Church, and to all those in the global sacred plant medicine community doing this work with integrity and care—you are the reason this path continues. Thank you for welcoming me with open arms. To Inti, for your grounded wisdom, your faith in the land, and the way you listened without needing to fix. You showed me that sacred paths often begin where language ends. To Rosalia, for your gentle teachings on energy, vibration, and truth. You gave me tools I didn't know I was allowed to hold. And to Chad, Alex, and all the brothers and sisters who sat in ceremony with me—you showed me that real strength looks like surrender.

To my wife, Erin, my love and quiet anchor. You witnessed every breath, every unraveling, and still chose to stay. I wouldn't have made it through without you. Thank you for reading every comma-heavy draft with patience and for gently reminding me that I don't need to pause quite so much. To my mother, Penny Sadler, who had the courage to let me tell this story honestly. Thank you for your strength, grace, and willingness to be seen through my eyes, even when it wasn't easy. To my late father, Kent J. Sadler, who prayed for me every single day—your steady faith was a lifeline I didn't always recognize, but one I always carried with me. To my niece, Danni, for your courage in carrying the weight of trauma, for battling through depression, and for continuing to take steps even when the path is unclear. May you find your own Middle Ground, and may your steps become prayers. To Pepper, my birth mother. You were fierce, complicated, and unafraid to chart your own course. I got more from you than I once believed—maybe even a knack for writing. And to my late brother, Spencer—your struggle changed me. Your absence continues to guide me.

To my mentors and friends from DSS and SAPD—you shaped the person who wrote these pages. I still carry deep respect for you, and I still carry the badge in my heart. And to everyone whose name I didn't mention: you know where you are in these pages. I love you, and I am grateful for you every day.

To Josh Banks, for taking on the first round of editing and helping me shape the bones of this story with skill and generosity. To Genet Jones, for her thoughtful eye and help bringing the final details into focus. And to my dear friends who read early drafts and offered raw, unfiltered feedback—your honesty and encouragement made this possible.

Lastly, to you, the reader—if you've made it this far, this story is yours too. Thank you for bearing witness. May your path lead you to peace, truth, and the remembering of who you are.

P.S. And also—to Joe Rogan and Graham Hancock and the conversations that planted the seed for this journey—you opened a door I didn't know existed. Thank you!

ABOUT THE AUTHOR

K. L. Sadler is a retired federal agent and first-time author. After a high-stress career shaped by duty and resilience, she turned inward to confront trauma, identity, and healing. Today she works to build bridges between the first responder community and the right to access traditional and ancient paths to healing, including ayahuasca. She is currently based in Brussels with her wife and three dogs.

Learn more at klsadler.com.

instagram.com/klsadler_

facebook.com/klsadler

linkedin.com/in/kemmisadler